(DO)UBLE KNIT (SPORT WORSTED)	ARAN	MOHAIR	CHUNKY (BULKY)	YARN TYPE:		
(4)mm–3½ mm 7–10 7–4	5½ mm–4 mm 5–8 9–5	6 mm–5 mm 4–6 10–8	7½ mm–5½ mm 1–5 10½–9	**NEEDLE SIZE: METRIC** UK US		
20–24 26–32	16–20 20–26	14–16 18–22	12–16 16–20	**STS** **ROWS**	**STOCKING/ STOCKINETTE STITCH**	
19–22 40–48	15–18 32–38	13–15 26–30	11–15 24–32	**STS** **ROWS**	**GARTER STITCH**	
20–24 32–40	16–20 26–34	14–16 22–30	12–16 20–28	**STS** **ROWS**	**MOSS STITCH**	
(4)mm–3 mm 8–11 6–2	5 mm–3¼ mm 6–10 8–3	5½ mm–4 mm 5–8 9–6	7 mm–4½ mm 2–7 10½–7	**NEEDLE SIZE: METRIC** UK US		
32–40 28–36	24–30 22–28	20–28 18–26	18–24 16–22	**STS** **ROWS**	**K1 P1 RIB UNSTRETCHED**	

- Rayon and viscose garments stretch if hung up, and take on the shape of hangers, hooks, etc.

- Cotton knits will regain their shape and suppleness if dryed in a tumble dryer.

- Press natural fibres with a damp cloth; never apply steam directly to the fabric.

- Check colour fastness of rich cotton yarns by washing strands beforehand; especially if a light background is used with dark colours or vice versa.

- Remove all trimmings like feathers, leather, fur, etc. before washing, unless they are colourfast and washable.

KNIT Design

KNIT
Design

Betty Barnden and Gabi Tubbs

M
MACMILLAN
LONDON

Published in association with **TIGERLILY LTD**

Editor: **Elsie Burch Donald**
Book Designers: **Anthony Lawrence and Hilly Beavan**
Technical Illustrations: **Elaine Franks**
Fashion Illustrations: **Sally Lecky-Thompson**
Colour Photography: **Peter Waldman**

First published in Great Britain 1987 by
MACMILLAN LONDON LIMITED
4 Little Essex Street London WC2R 3LF
and Basingstoke

Associated companies in Auckland, Delhi, Dublin,
Caborone, Hamburg, Harare, Hong Kong, Johannesburg,
Kuala Lumpur, Lagos, Manzini, Melbourne, Mexico City,
Nairobi, New York, Singapore and Tokyo

British Library Cataloguing in Publication Data

Tubbs, Gabi
   Knitting & design.
   1. Knitting
   I. Title   II. Barnden, Betty
   746.43'2   TT820

ISBN 0-333-44001-3

Typeset by Rowland Phototypesetting Limited,
Bury St Edmunds, Suffolk

Printed in Italy

CONTENTS

INTRODUCTION

Knitting is like cooking in that precise instructions are normal to both crafts, and usually it takes confidence or considerable desperation to deviate. We may replace sage with thyme because we are out of sage, or one brand of knitting yarn with another because the recommended one is discontinued, but the results are always hit and miss, full of hazards, uncertainties and – occasionally – some marvellous results. It is entirely a matter of luck, and it is possible to cook or knit all of one's life without ever glimpsing the underlying structure on which each craft is built, following instructions as if each recipe or pattern were a detached entity with no connection to any other recipe or pattern. However, once the underlying structure has been exposed and grasped, it becomes possible to reassemble the whole edifice to suit us.

For in knitting, as in cooking, there *is* an underlying structure – a method for getting where we want to go – in other words, building up knitted fabric into a desired shape and size. This book's purpose is to expose that structure and free knitters from the inevitable confines of step-by-step patterns with their inherent limitations on size, yarn, stitch pattern and so on.

UNDERLYING STRUCTURE

Knitted fabric is normally shaped by decreasing stitches as we work in order to make fabric narrower, or increasing stitches to make the fabric wider. Looked at this way design becomes a very simple and straightforward business. We only need to know how much wider or narrower to make the fabric as we go along. To do this we need to know the correct garment measurements and – most importantly – find out how many stitches (or rows) it will take to arrive at the measurements which we want. This is accomplished by simple formulae based on the tension/gauge. And that, basically, is all there is to it, but a good eye and knitting experience always help.

USING THIS BOOK

The book is divided into three main categories which are interlocking. First, the basics: knitting techniques, the all-important subjects of correct measurements, 'ease', tension/gauge, and how to increase and decrease stitches to make fabric wider or narrower.

Second: illustrated step-by-step patterns. These may seem at first glance out of place in a book about designing new patterns, but not so. The patterns can of course be knitted as they appear, but they can also be used as templates on which to base other designs, or for modified versions using different yarns and stitches, altering the neckline or sleeve length but keeping the overall shape. All the patterns have been specially arranged to facilitate this.

The third component is design, and in addition to information and advice about colour, texture and stitch patterns, are the instructions how to calculate all parts of a garment, combine them to suit one's own taste, and knit them to the correct measurements.

6

Sampler cushions illustrate how different stitch patterns create a variety of subtle textures pleasing to the eye. These are worked in the following patterns (lower left to upper right): shadow, feather and fan, scroll, Irish moss diamond, and twisted cable. The method for knitting each one appears in the Stitch Library.

The cushions are knitted in cotton and silk from a range of standard double knitting/worsted yarns from the Pingouin range.

Each cushion takes between 3–5 50g balls and is knitted on 4mm needles (UK8, US 5–6).

To work out a cushion design of your own, see page 65 for calculating the number of stitches and rows needed for your cushion measurements.

MEASURING

Measuring is the key to a garment that fits properly. Printed knitting patterns usually fit a short range of standard sizes, but with the information in this book you can learn to adapt them to fit other sizes, or alter a given style.

To work out your own patterns, accurate measuring before you begin is crucial.

Inches and centimetres. Many knitting patterns give measurements in both inches and centimetres. Use whichever system you prefer, but always stick to the same one. That way you will not make a mistake in measuring and end up with for example armholes that are far too small. Also the two systems of measurement do not always correspond: 4″ is approximately equal to 10cm, but if you look at a tape measure marked in both inches and centimetres you will see that 12″ is 30.5cm, 20″ is 41cm, and so on.

All measurements in this book are in inches.

EASE

In addition to the bust/chest size, many knitting patterns now state the actual measurement of the garment. The difference between the two is called 'ease'. It is necessary for freedom of movement. (Really tight fitting garments, such as skinny rib sweaters, are usually made in stretchy stitches.)

The amount of ease will vary according to the style of the garment. Two inches added to the bust/chest size is a minimum amount for a classic fit sweater, under which only a light blouse or T-shirt might be worn. Four inches would give a looser fit for a more sporty garment or a cardigan style: 6 inches or 8 inches for a loose, over-size style.

Other measurements such as width of sleeves and depth of armholes also allow for ease.

A rule of thumb reference guide is given opposite.

MEASURING A GARMENT

An interesting exercise in order to understand ease more thoroughly is to measure one of your own sweaters, as in fig. 1, and then take your body measurements and compare the two different sets of measurements – you may be surprised at the difference.

Measuring an existing gar-

For a classic fit, add the following ease allowance to body measurements. For a looser style, add more – perhaps twice as much.

EASE CHART	Child 22″–28″ chest	Woman 30″–38″ chest	Man 36″–40″ chest
To chest measurement A add minimum of	2″	2″–3″	2″–3″
To round neck measurement D add minimum of	2″–3″	2″–3″	2″–3″
To round shoulder N, add minimum of	I″	I″–2″	2″–3″
To round arm measurement O (at armhole level) add	I½″–2″	2″–3″	2″–3″
To hip measurement S, add minimum of	2″	2″	—

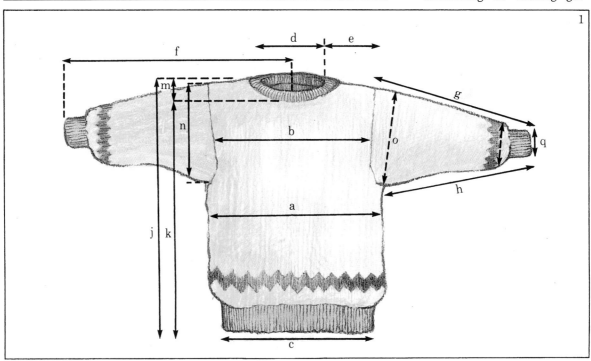

1

ment can be very useful too in providing a guideline for making another similar sweater using a different yarn or stitch pattern.

Lay the garment *flat* on the table (or the carpet), with seams straight and matching. Use a tape measure, and record the measurements from fig. 1 which are listed below.

a – chest width
b – shoulder to shoulder width
c – welt width
d – back neck width
e – shoulder width
f – centre back to cuff
g – shoulder seam to cuff
h – underarm to cuff
j – centre back length
k – centre front length
m – neck opening depth (= j minus k)
n – armhole depth
o – sleeve width at armhole
p – sleeve width just above cuff
q – cuff width

Note that most of these measurements are taken straight – either parallel with the lower edge or vertical to it. A common mistake is to measure round the curve of an armhole; this is wrong. The depth of an armhole is taken vertically.

Of course, some of these measurements need to be doubled before they can be compared with body measurements: chest width (a), welt width (c), sleeve width at armhole (o), sleeve width just above cuff (p) and cuff width (q).

Measuring the body

It is quite difficult to measure yourself – you really need someone to help you.

Always take measurements *over* the same amount of clothes you intend to wear under the garment you wish to make. For a coat or jacket this is terribly important.

Take measurements with the body in a relaxed, upright position.

Figure 2
a – bust or chest. Measure round the fullest part of the bust. Children and men should be measured with the chest expanded. Add ease as required.
b – shoulder to shoulder (taken across the back). Necessary for set-in sleeves. Compare with

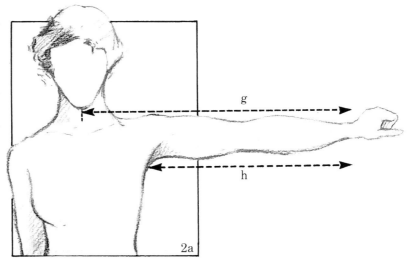

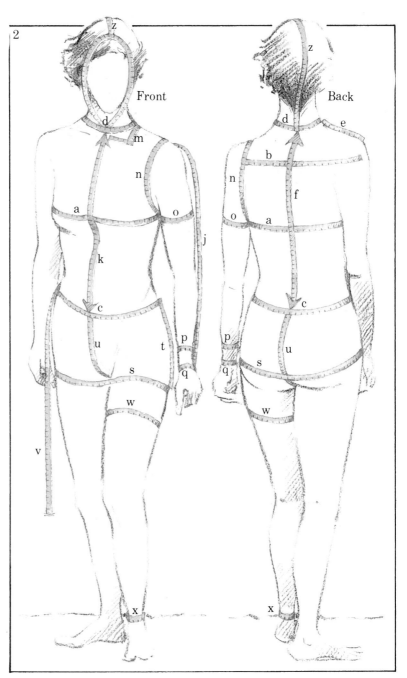

the measurement on an existing garment that fits well.

c – welt. Measure round the body at the length you wish the garment to reach. Add ease as required.

d – round neck. Measure right round the neck at the appropriate height. Add ease as required.

e – shoulder. From level of neck measurement (d) to point of shoulder (for set-in sleeves).

f – centre back length. From base of neck to length required.

g – with arm extended, from centre back neck to cuff. Particularly useful for T-shaped or drop-shoulder shapes (fig. 2a).

h – from underarm to cuff. Actual body measurement will be *longer* than sweater measurement, the amount depending on the style.

j – from point of shoulder to cuff. For set-in sleeves.

k – centre front. Length from lowest point of round neck measurement (d) to length required.

m – depth of front neck opening. Usually the difference between centre back length (f) and centre front length (k).

n – round shoulder measurement. Measure right round the shoulder, passing the tape under arm and back to point of

shoulder. Tape should not restrict arm movement. Very useful for checking set-in sleeves, and also other shoulder shapes. Add ease as required.

o – measure round arm at underarm level. Add ease as required.

p – measure round lower arm just above level of cuff. Add ease as required.

q – measure round wrist. Add ease to make cuff wide enough to stretch over hand.

r – waist. Measure round natural waistline. Necessary for skirts and trousers. Add ease as required.

s – hip. Measure round fullest part. For skirts and trousers and also long jackets or tops. Add ease as required.

t – hip depth. From level of waist to level of hip measurement measured down side of body as shown. For skirts, trousers, long jackets or tops.

u – crotch. From centre-front waist to centre-back waist, between legs. Only necessary for trousers. Add ease as required.

v – skirt length. From level of waist to length required measured down side of body as shown. Allow tape to hang from waist while wearing a similar skirt and appropriate shoes.

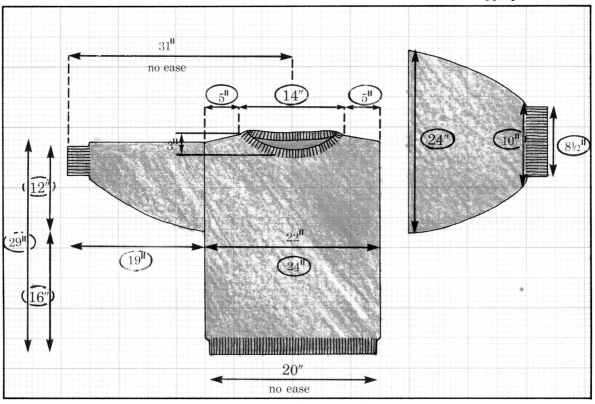

w – thigh. Measure round fullest part. Only necessary for trousers. Add ease as required.

x – ankle. For trousers with cuffs, e.g. for babies. Add ease to make cuff wide enough to stretch over foot.

y – round face. Lowest point on neck-line required. For hoods – as tight as you wish.

z – forehead to neck. From highest point of y to centre back of neckline required. For hoods.

DIAGRAM

When planning a design or adapting an existing pattern, it is necessary to draw a diagram of the garment pieces as they would be laid out flat (fig. 1 opposite). This diagram does not need to be to scale but it is quite useful to use squared paper (as shown) to give an approximate idea of proportions. For each measurement line, write down on the diagram the actual body measurement.

Where ease is added, or length adjustments made, write the garment measurement in a different colour (or circled).

It is by converting these measurements into the numbers of stitches and rows it will take to fill the required space that knitting patterns are developed. The simple formulae involved are explained on page 65.

MEASURING KNITTING IN PROGRESS

Measuring the *width* of work in progress is often inaccurate because the measurements may alter when work is pressed or blocked. Also, if the work is still on needles it is not always possible to lay it flat. This is why the tension/gauge square (page 12) is so important and why it should always be pressed or blocked before measuring. If the tension/gauge is accurate, you can proceed with confidence.

However, as a rough guide you can check the width as follows: work to the middle of a row (leaving an equal number of stitches on each needle). Lay the piece *flat* and measure width.

Measure length from underside of needle to lower edge. DO NOT

STRETCH the knitting (especially lengthwise). Wishful thinking does not work!

Most patterns give lengthwise measurements from the cast on edge.

Always measure the depth of an armhole (set-in sleeve fig. 1, or raglan fig. 2) with the tape measure vertical as shown – never along the curve or slope.

Always measure the length of a sleeve at the centre, never along an increased edge (fig. 3).

Measuring bands or collars knitted as a length. When knitting, for instance, a cardigan with separate bands sewn round the front and neck edge, the instructions often say 'work until band matches length round neck edge'. There is an accurate way to do this.

Join the shoulder seams of the garment. Begin to knit the band as instructed (usually beginning with buttonhole part). After working several inches, sew the band to the front edge of the garment (fig. 4) stretching just slightly so that it lies flat but not so tightly that the edge is pulled shorter than the rest of the garment (see seams, page 16).

Continue knitting and sewing a few inches at a time until band fits. Cast off.

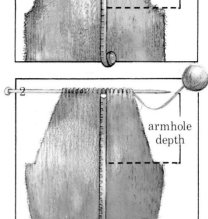

armhole depth

armhole depth

sleeve length taken at centre

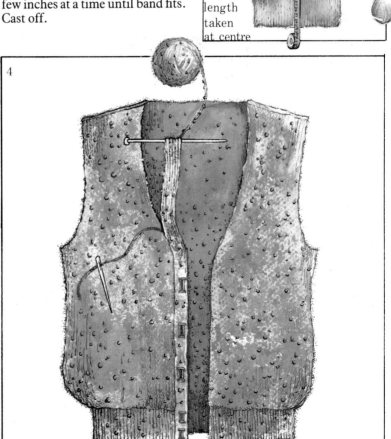

OMNIBUS ESSENTIALS

There are two basic knitting stitches – knit and purl; and even the most exotic textures are variations of them. It is the choice of stitch and yarn plus the diameter of the knitting needles that combine to form all knitted fabrics. There remains only the shape into which they are knitted.

TENSION/GAUGE

This refers to the number of stitches and the number of rows it takes to knit a given measurement – usually 4″ square since smaller pieces are less accurate and more difficult to measure. Every knitting pattern states the correct tension/gauge using the size of needles, type of yarn and stitch called for in the pattern. For example: 28 sts and 34 rows to 4″ using 2mm/UK 14/US 0 needles.

Correct tension/gauge is crucially important in order to make the finished garment the right size. The effect of even a small variation in tension will be cumulative. If your own tension/gauge square is smaller than that stated in the pattern it means you are working too tightly. Change to a size larger needles and test again. Conversely, if the square measures too big, try smaller needles.

If you elect to use a different combination of stitch/yarn/needles than that which is stipulated, or you wish to work out a design of your own, then you must find out the tension/gauge for your own combination over a 4″ square measurement and you must make a tension/gauge square for all areas which have different stitch patterns, e.g. ribbed edgings.

A tension/gauge chart at the back of this book provides a useful reference for combining a variety of different yarns, needles and stitches, but since no two people knit exactly alike it is *always* necessary to check your own tension/gauge against that designated.

Measuring tension/gauge

Press or block the knitted square in the same way as you intend to treat the finished garment (see Assembly, page 18). Do not press rib samples.

Allow swatches to dry thoroughly. Unpin and if possible leave for a few hours to take up a natural position.

To measure stitches, lay swatch right side up on a flat surface and insert two pins (fig. 1) between vertical rows of stitches exactly 4″ apart. Use a flat ruler.

Count the number of stitches and half stitches (if any) between the pins. Fig. 1 shows 10½ stitches between the pins.

To measure rows, place pins horizontally, measuring with the ruler straight up a line of stitches and counting the rows between them (fig. 2). For some stitch patterns, e.g. st st, it is easier to measure rows on the wrong side.

Ribbing tension/gauge samples should be measured with the rib swatch stretched as much as you want it to be stretched in use. For a tight-fitting waistband stretch it a fair amount but not as far as it will go; for a cardigan button band, stretch it very slightly or the edge will curl.

Terminology

A list of knitting abbreviations used in knitting patterns appears in the front of this book. Throughout the text all measurements are given in inches.

UK/USA terminology. Most knitting terms are the same in both countries. Where they are different the UK term is given first. For example, cast/bind off, tension/gauge. The size of knitting needles (see chart in front of book) and the general descriptions of yarns are also different.

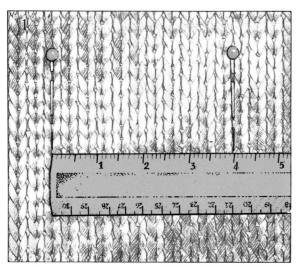

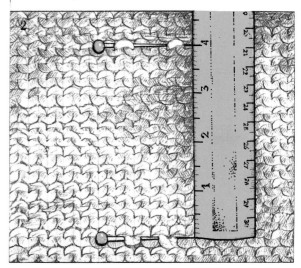

CASTING ON

Two methods are given below: the thumb method is easier to do but the two-needle style makes for a more elastic edge.

Thumb method

Make a slip knot about 1 yard from yarn end. This is a stitch.

Hold the needle in your right hand and the shorter length of yarn in your left hand, securing it against palm as shown in fig. 1.

Insert needle under secured yarn, then wind yarn *from ball* under and over the point of the needle (fig. 2) and draw the needle towards you and through the loop on your thumb, (fig. 3). This makes the next stitch (fig. 4).

Two needle method

Make a slip knot on left-hand needle (fig. 1).

Insert right-hand needle into slip knot from front to back and wind the yarn under and over the point of right-hand needle (fig. 2).

Draw the right-hand needle and yarn forward through slip knot (fig. 3).

Transfer the loop now on right-hand needle to left-hand needle.

Insert right-hand needle between two loops now on left-hand needle (fig. 4).

Wind yarn under and over the point of right-hand needle, as in fig. 2; draw loop through (fig. 3).

Transfer new loop to left-hand needle as before and continue.

KNIT STITCH

Hold needle with cast-on stitches in your left hand. Insert right-hand needle from *front to back* into first stitch (fig. 1).

Loop yarn round point of needle (fig. 2) from *behind*.

Draw right-hand needle forward through cast-on stitch (fig. 3).

Pull right-hand needle to the right to slip off old stitch (fig. 4), leaving new stitch on right-hand needle.

To complete one row, repeat these steps with each cast-on stitch.

To knit next row, swap needles so that knitting is in left hand, and continue as described above.

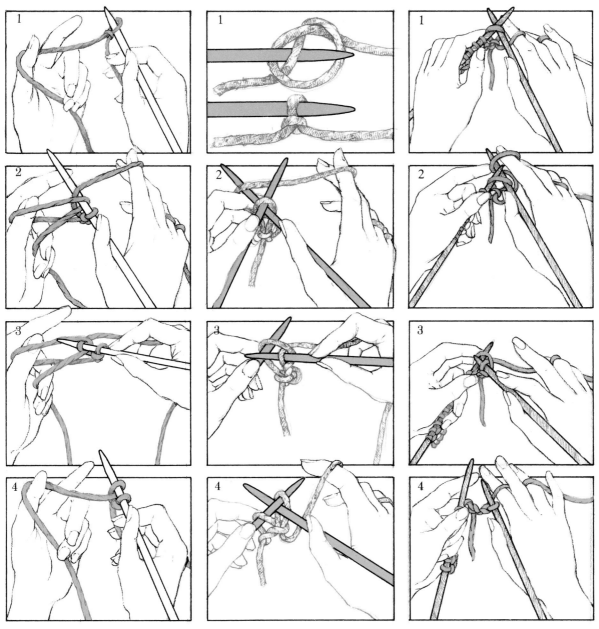

PURL STITCH

Keep yarn in front. Slip needle into stitch *from behind*, looping yarn round needle (fig. 1), and draw it through stitch now on both needles to right needle (fig. 2). Old stitch slips off left needle (fig. 3).

INCREASING

Increases (making extra stitches) are used when shaping a garment, e.g. to widen part of a sleeve, and also as part of stitch patterns, such as lacy patterns, when they are normally balanced by corresponding decreases.

Yarn round needle increases (fig. 1) are the simplest method of increasing. The yarn is looped round the needle point; this gives a rather uneven edge which can be hidden by a seam. Used in mid-row, this will make a hole as for lace. Be sure when working in mid-row in K or P to loop the yarn anti-clockwise in such a way as to make an extra loop (unless otherwise stated in the pattern).

Working twice in one stitch (fig. 2). This leaves a small neat hole which is acceptable for shaped edges.

Knit a stitch without slipping it off the needle. Then knit a second stitch into the *back* of the stitch. Slip old stitch off needle.

Invisible increases are a very good method for working shapings.

Insert left needle from front to back under the horizontal strand lying between 2 stitches (fig. 3).

On a K row, knit into the *back* of the strand (fig. 4). This twists the stitch, making the result invisible.

On a P row, purl into the back of the strand (fig. 5).

Sloping increases

This method gives the possibility of pairing increases, sloping to left and right, and is therefore particularly suitable for 'darts' and shaping highly tailored garments. Sleeve edges, for example, can be sloped (to the right on right-hand edge and left on left-hand edge) to give a very neat finish. The increase is made by working into the loop below a stitch as well as the stitch itself, as follows:

Sloping to right (fig. 6), knit into loop below next stitch, then knit the stitch.

Sloping to left (fig. 7), insert needle into loop below last completed stitch, pull back gently and knit the loop.

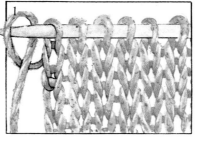

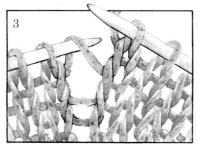

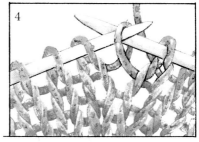

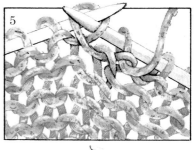

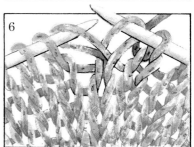

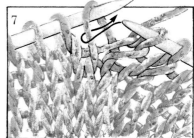

DECREASING

Like increases, decreases are used to shape a garment or as part of a stitch pattern when they are balanced by corresponding increases.

Different methods of decreasing will make the stitches slope to the left or to the right. Normally when shaping a piece of knitting, the stitches are decreased so that the slope of the stitches follows the slope of the edge. For instance, when shaping a sleeve the decreasing stitches slope towards the centre, whereas when shaping a V neck they slope outwards from the centre towards the shoulders.

K decrease sloping left (sl1, k1, psso). Slip one stitch knitwise, K next stitch (fig. 1), pass slip stitch over (fig. 2). Use on right hand edge of work.

K decrease sloping right (k2 tog). Knit two stitches together through the *front* of both loops. Use on left hand edge of work.

P decrease sloping right (on st st side). Purl two stitches together.

P. decrease sloping left (on st st side). Purl two stitches together through the back loops.

Double decreases

Sometimes it is necessary to decrease by two stitches at the same time, for instance at the top of raglan sleeves.

Double decrease sloping right (k3 tog). Knit three stitches together through front loops.

Double decrease sloping left. Knit three stitches together through back loops *or* slip one stitch knitwise, K next two stitches together, pass slip stitch over. (The first method is sometimes rather tight.)

Double decrease vertical (fig. 3). This method makes a line in the work sloping neither right nor left. Slip two stitches inserting needle knitwise into second stitch, then into first stitch; K next stitch then pass the two slip stitches over. Use to make 'dart' shapings such as in a waisted jacket or a skirt.

CASTING/ BINDING OFF

Knit two stitches loosely. Then, using the tip of the left-hand needle, slip the first stitch over the second (fig. 1).

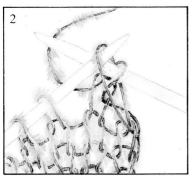

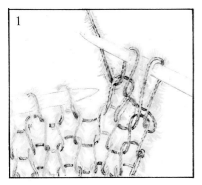

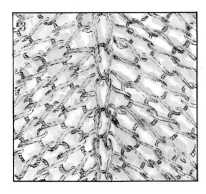

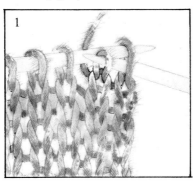

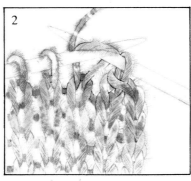

Knit another stitch loosely (fig. 2) and slip previous stitch over it. Continue to last stitch but one, cut yarn and draw end back through last stitch.

Always cast/bind off in the pattern worked. To cast/bind off ribbing, knit the knit stitches and purl the purl stitches.

READING A PATTERN

Knitting patterns contain detailed stitch-by-stitch instructions set out according to certain developed conventions, such as the use of abbreviations, a list of which appears in the front of this book.

Sizes. When instructions give different sizes, the smallest size is given first and the subsequent ones are in parentheses, e.g. 32 (34, 36, 38). Relevant instructions will fall accordingly throughout the pattern, so that k3 (4, 5, 6) means to knit 3 stitches for size 32, 4 stitches for size 34, and so on. The knitter must of course follow instructions for one size throughout the pattern. Where there is only one set of figures, it applies to all sizes.

Special terms

Square brackets means to repeat instructions inside brackets as many times as indicated, e.g. [k1, p1] twice.

An asterisk is also used to mark off a repeat section of a pattern, e.g. *p4, k2, rep from * to end.

Knitwise (purlwise). Insert needle into the next stitch as if about to knit (purl).

Pick up and knit (see page 16).

Adapting patterns. The step-by-step patterns given in this book also contain in italics an overall instruction so that the pattern can be adjusted or restyled to suit personal preference.

ATTACHING NEW YARN

Never tie a new thread on in the middle of a piece of work. It will probably show. Instead, join at the outer edge of work.

Make a slip knot with the new strand around the working strand, then move the slip knot up to edge of work and continue knitting.

To avoid running out of yarn in the middle of a row, tie a slip knot at centre of remaining yarn when you think you have enough left for 2 rows. Work one row. If you do not reach the knot, you have enough left for the second row. (Undo the knot.)

SPECIAL TECHNIQUES

The techniques described in this section are useful to knitters of all levels, not just for those with long experience.

PICK UP AND KNIT

This technique is used to pick up stitches along the edge of knitted fabric, as when beginning a neckband.

For a neat finish begin with right side of work facing and insert needle one whole stitch (two threads) in from the edge (figs. 1 and 2), loop yarn round needle and pull the yarn through to make a stitch.

Always space the picked up stitches evenly. For instance, if you need to pick up 36 stitches evenly from a neck edge, divide the edge into four equal sections with pins and pick up and knit 9 stitches from each section.

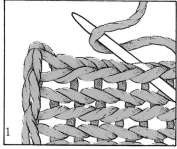

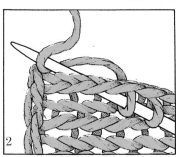

SELVEDGES

A selvedge is a narrow border worked at side edges, *in addition to pattern stitches*. Its purpose is to make a neater more professional edge for seams, and to prevent curling.

The most useful selvedge is to knit one stitch more than the pattern calls for on each straight edge which will be seamed. Always knit a *knit* stitch no matter what type of stitch is on the rest of the row. This is taken into the seam.

16

CALCULATING YARN

If you wish to knit a pattern in a yarn other than specified, or to calculate yarn for a design of your own, see the chart at the front of the book for reference. However, if you are working in a complicated stitch pattern, or desire, for whatever reason, a more accurate calculation, use the following method:

Knit one complete ball of the yarn you intend using to make a rectangle in the stitch and tension/gauge required.

Then calculate the area of the rectangle. If, for instance, it is 8″ wide and 10″ long, the area will be 80 square inches (8 × 10 = 80).

Next, calculate roughly the area of all the pieces to be knitted, not forgetting collar, pocket linings, etc.

Supposing your total area is 640 square inches, then to find out the total yarn requirement, divide 640 (the square inches in the garment) by 80 (the square inches in one ball). The answer in this case would be 8 balls of yarn in all.

Always be generous when approximating yarn quantities.

CIRCULAR KNITTING

Circular knitting is used to make a seamless tube which may be the body of a garment, the sleeves, the trouser legs or just the neckband of a sweater. It is a particularly neat method for neckbands. It may be worked with a circular needle, or a set of double-pointed needles.

Circular needles are available in different lengths and diameters. The length should be at least 2″ shorter than the circumference of the knitting so that the stitches fit without stretching. (Very small tubes must therefore be knitted on double-pointed needles.)

Cast on number of stitches as required and then join into a circle (fig. 1), placing a marking ring or loop of contrast thread on right-hand needle at start of first round; this marker is slipped from left needle to right needle every round to make counting the completed rounds easier. Make sure the cast-on stitches are not twisted around the needle as a twisted edge cannot

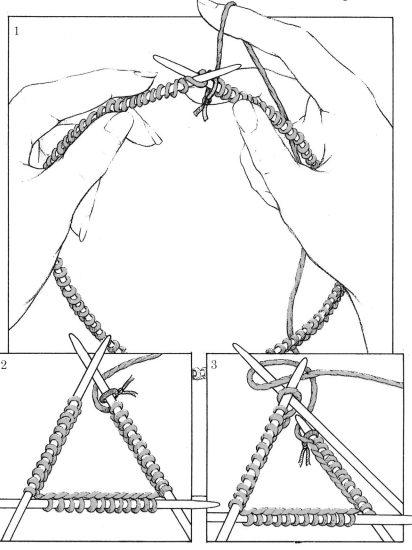

be corrected later.

Circular needles can also be used to knit a flat piece and are particularly useful for large projects with many stitches. In this case, after casting on, turn the work *without* joining into a circle, and turn on every row.

Double-pointed needles are usually sold in sets of four, but five or more may be used if necessary for large pieces.

To make a tube with four double-pointed needles, cast on one third of the total number onto each of three needles as fig. 2 and place a ring marker or loop of contrast yarn on last needle after last cast-on stitch. Lay the three needles in a triangle as shown, with all stitches untwisted.

Using the fourth needle, work into the first cast-on stitch (fig. 3), thus joining the work into a circle, and work all stitches on first needle. The first needle is now empty, so use it to work the stitches from the second needle, and so on. Slip the marker on every round to make easier the counting of rows and changes in pattern.

WORKING CABLES

To work cables, you need a cable needle, which is a short double-pointed needle, of similar size to the main needles. (It should not be bigger or the stitches will be stretched; if it is too small it will slip out of the stitches.)

A simple cable usually consists of an even number of stitches, e.g. 4, 6 or 8. Half of these stitches will be twisted over or under the other half.

Cable twisting to the right. Slip first half of cable stitches on cable needle and hold at back of work (fig. 1); knit second half of cable stitches, then knit stitches from cable needle (fig. 2).

Cable twisting to left. Slip first half of cable stitches on cable needle and hold at front of work (fig. 3); knit second half of cable stitches then knit stitches from cable needle.

There are many stitch patterns using cabling, and many different forms of cables, but they are all based on these two methods of twisting the stitches.

SWISS DARNING

This is a form of embroidery which can be used to add small areas of colour to a garment (fig. 1), or small details to a picture knit (such as eyes or mouth), or even to correct a mistake in fairisle knitting.

However, Swiss darning does result in a double thickness of fabric, so it is not really advisable over large areas as the final effect may be rather stiff and heavy.

Any yarn can be used, but it is best to use one of the same weight (or slightly thicker) than the background, in order to cover the knitted stitches properly.

Start at the bottom right-hand corner of the area to be Swiss darned. Leave long ends at the back to be run in afterwards.

Insert needle (use a blunt-ended needle) from back of work at base of first stitch to be covered and pull yarn through to the front.

Pass needle under the two loops of the same stitch one row above, from right to left; pull the yarn through and re-insert the needle at the base of the same stitch. Pull yarn through to back of work (fig. 2).

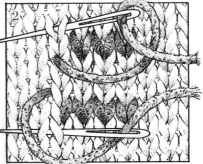

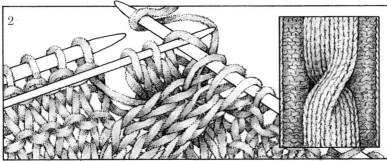

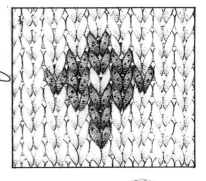

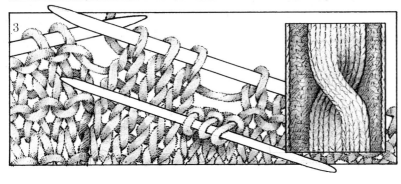

Work along the first row from right to left, and the row above from left to right, inserting the needle under the two loops from left to right on this second row. Keep each stitch the same tension as the stitch beneath.

Run ends in at back of work, within darned area.

CORRECTING ERRORS

Sometimes it is easier to correct a mistake or dropped stitch without unpicking several rows. Look closely at the way each K and P stitch is formed and you will see how the position of the yarn may be changed using a crochet hook.

In stocking/stockinette stitch, insert hook front to back, hook it over horizontal thread and draw through loop on hook (fig. 1).

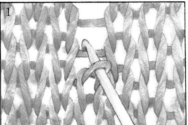

In garter stitch the dropped stitch is worked from one side and then the other. With right side facing, insert hook front to back in each 'knit' loop and pull through (fig. 2); for a 'purl' loop, insert hook from back to front (fig. 3), hooking it *over* the horizontal thread, and pull through.

Note: Be sure to transfer stitch to needle twisted in the same way as the rest of the row.

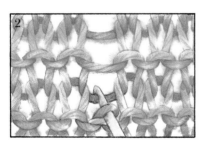

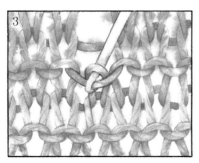

Unravelling. If you do need to unravel several rows, mark the row in which the error was made with a piece of contrast yarn. Unravel to one row above the marked row.

Hold work so that end of yarn is on left. Hold needle in left hand. With yarn behind work, insert needle into a knit stitch as fig. 4

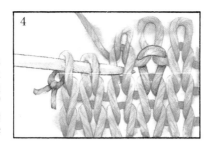

and pull out the stitch above; to unpick a purl stitch insert needle as in fig. 5.

ASSEMBLY

For a professional finish it is advisable to 'block' pieces before sewing them together. The type of seam used to sew them together will vary according to different parts of the garment.

BLOCKING

You need a large flat surface for this. If you can block all pieces at the same time, you will not only save time but will be able to match the measurements more easily. Plywood or hardboard covered with one or more layers of blanket material, stretched and stapled down round the edges, makes a good surface. Your ironing board will do for small pieces.

A dry iron and a damp cloth is preferable to a steam iron because the effect is more uniform. *Never* use any iron directly on knitting.

First weave in all loose ends on each piece (fig. 1), then lay piece wrong side up on padded surface and adjust measurements as required. Natural fibre yarns may be slightly stretched to make the garment larger. Fairisle or similar patterns may need to be stretched widthwise to gain correct measurements.

Pin the corners first, then pin along edges, inserting pins at right angles to edges. Be sure to use enough pins so that the edges are not scalloped. Do *not* pin rib edges.

Consult yarn ball band for pressing instructions. If in doubt, test your tension/gauge swatch first.

Wool and other natural fibres in flat stitches. Use a cotton or linen cloth (a well-washed tea towel is ideal), wet it and wring it out hard. Place cloth over knitting (omit ribbing) and hold the iron over each area in turn – do not press hard with the iron or move it about on the surface; the object is to let the steam enter the knitting, not to press it flat. Leave pinned out until dry.

For textured stitches and synthetic/natural mixtures apply no pressure at all, but hold the iron hovering just on the surface of the cloth. Leave pinned out until dry.

For synthetic yarns do not use any heat. Lay a wet cloth over each piece and leave until dry. Alternatively spray thoroughly with clean water using a plant spray or similar and leave to dry.

SEAMS

Always use a blunt-ended needle for seams to avoid splitting stitches. Special knitters' sewing-up needles are available in different sizes to suit different thicknesses of yarn. Use the same yarn as the knitting. Chunky/bulky yarns may be split so that just one strand is used. Bouclé or knobbly yarns are sometimes impossible to sew with; use a matching colour in a smooth yarn, if possible in a similar fibre to avoid washing problems.

Invisible seam. This seam (fig. 1) is usually worked one stitch in from each edge (see selvedge page

16) and makes it possible to match stripes and other patterns exactly, as it is worked with right sides facing. Yarn should be pulled quite tightly, but not so tightly that the seam puckers. Use this seam for side and sleeve seams where a really neat finish is required.

Shoulder seam (fig. 2), a similar seam to fig. 3, but worked across cast-on or cast/bound off edges with right sides facing, as shown.

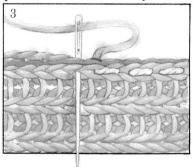

Ribbing – side seam (fig. 3), worked with wrong sides together. Corresponding stitches from each piece should match exactly.

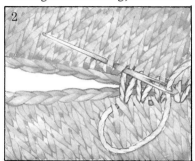

Grafted seam. This is a seam that actually makes a row of stitches indistinguishable from knitted stitches without any lumpy edge. Two open edges may be grafted together, for instance shoulders, either working from two needles or with the knitted loops threaded on 2 lengths of contrasting smooth yarn before grafting.

How to graft. Both edges must have the same number of stitches. Use a large blunt-ended needle to avoid splitting stitches.

With the two pieces right side up, bring the needle up through lower and upper end stitches (fig. 4). *Insert knitwise through lower stitch where thread comes out and purlwise through next lower stitch. Insert knitwise through upper stitch where thread comes out, purlwise through next upper stitch.*

Repeat * to *, pulling thread to same tension as rest of work,

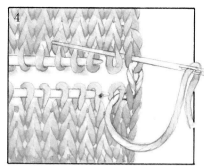

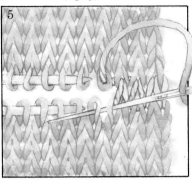

slipping stitches off needles as they are worked (fig. 5).

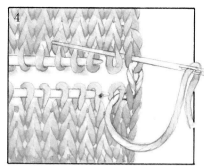

If stitches are held on a contrast thread, pull this out when grafting is complete.

Drop-shoulder sleeves, where the top edge of the sleeve is unshaped, should be joined by combining the methods in figs. 1 and 2, since a cast/bound off edge is being attached to a side edge. The number of stitches on the sleeve is usually less than the number of rows they are to fit, so the extra rows should be worked in evenly across the seam.

Raglan shaping seams are usually joined by the invisible method (fig. 1) which can be particularly neat and effective if the decreasings are worked a few stitches in from each edge to form a decorative band either side of the seam. The number of rows should match exactly.

Set-in sleeves Always join side and shoulder sleeve seams first. The sleeve cap is curved differently from the armhole and is often slightly larger.

Mark centre of sleeve cap with a pin, and place two more pins, one each side half way between centre and underarm seam.

On main part of garment, place pins at shoulder and half way between shoulder and side seams.

Place sleeve inside garment with right sides together so that pins match; pin in position round edge, taking up any surplus evenly on sleeve edge. Sew with firm backstitch.

FINAL PRESSING

If required, the garment may be given a final pressing using iron and dry or damp cloth (according to ball band or type of fibre), paying particular attention to seams.

FITTING A ZIP

The edges of the knitting should never be stretched along a zip – the result will be a crinkled zip. Edges which have knitted selvedges (page 16) will look very neat and professional.

Choose a zip exactly to the length or up to ½″ shorter than the edges of the opening.

With zip closed, pin one edge of the knitting to the zip, spreading any excess length evenly, as close to the teeth as possible but not overlapping them or the zip will catch when opened. *Do not stretch the edge.* Tack in position.

Pin other edge in same way, matching any pattern, stripes etc. exactly, and tack in position.

Using matching yarn and a sharp-pointed darning needle, work a firm line of backstitch ½ or 1 stitch in from edge.

LINING

Sometimes it is an advantage to line a knitted garment, e.g. a jacket to make it windproof, or a skirt to keep its shape.

Press or block the knitted pieces as described above, then pin them to the lining material in the same way as the pieces of a paper dress pattern, i.e. straight with grain of fabric.

Cut out the pieces leaving a ⅝″ seam allowance all round, and join main seams as for a fabric garment.

Make up the knitted pieces.

Place lining inside knitting, wrong sides together, pin in position.

Turn in seam allowance at neck/front edges/waist; darts or pleats may be made at neck/waist if necessary. Slip stitch in position.

At lower edges of body/sleeve, linings are left unattached on heavier garments: turn up a hem on the lining to just short of length of knitting. On more finely textured cardigans for instance, slip stitch lining just above ribbed welt/border and, unless the lining is sleeveless, above ribbing on cuff.

ADAPTING PATTERN MEASUREMENTS

One obvious way to make a garment bigger all over than a given pattern is to use larger needles, thus working to a looser tension/gauge. Beware. Test your tension carefully before doing this. Most patterns use a tension/gauge which is best for that particular yarn and style, and if the tension/gauge square is loose and floppy, the garment will be too. It will drop in wear (and in the wash) and lose its shape very easily.

However, with a little thought and calculation, patterns can often be adapted using one of the methods below.

The first step is always to take body measurements and make a sketch diagram (see page 10). Compare these measurements with those given on the pattern. And read the pattern carefully.

ADJUSTING LENGTH

This is usually a matter of simply working more or less length *before* armhole shaping begins. (If you work more, or less, length into the armhole itself, you may find the sleeves don't fit.)

If the length on the pattern is determined by the number of rows worked over a stitch pattern, add or subtract one (or more) *whole pattern repeats* in order to begin armhole shaping on the same row. If the side seams are shaped by increasing up to the armholes, you may wish to redistribute these increases evenly by working more (or fewer) rows between them in order to gain the correct number of stitches to work armhole and neck shapings as given.

Adjusting sleeve length. Adjust sleeve length in the same way as body length. Making sleeves shorter often means working the increases more closely together.

ADJUSTING WIDTH

This is more difficult to do, particularly on patterns with complicated neck or armhole shapings such as raglan sleeves or V necks.

If you simply wish to increase the body width, you must decide whether extra decreases will be worked at the armholes so that the garment above the armholes will be the same as the pattern you are altering. This last sounds the easiest solution – until you come to fit the sleeves.

The decision really should be made with the shape of the wearer in mind. For instance, in adapting a pattern to fit a large man, consider his build and measure his neck and shoulders. Would he prefer a slightly wide neckline? If he will wear a shirt underneath, this is an easy solution:

Note: The adjustments below may be worked in reverse to decrease garment size.

Adjusting width at centre (fig. 1). Suppose your tension/gauge measures 20 stitches (and 26 rows) to 4″ and you wish to make the body of the sweater 4″ larger than the size given on a pattern. You would add 2″ (10 stitches) to the back width and the same amount to the front.

If there is a stitch pattern repeating over, say, 6 stitches, then you will have to adjust the number of extra stitches accordingly – in the above case, 12 stitches on back (or front) instead of 10. But if you do not want the lower edge to be so wide you might only add 6 stitches to the rib and increase the other 6 stitches across the top of the rib (see Increasing, page 14).

Add these 12 stitches all the way up the pattern: to the stitches remaining after armhole shaping, to the centre front and centre back neck stitches, and to the neckband stitches (24 in all). You could decrease a few stitches across the neck stitches when picking up for the neckband (page 77), but if you decrease too many you will get a gathered effect. This method is most suitable for raglan shapes to avoid re-calculating decreases.

Adding width at shoulders. Another option is to distribute the increased stitches between the two shoulders (fig. 2). This is a good way to work if the neck shape is complicated, because if you have to decrease more stitches on the V neck in the example shown, you might need more rows to fit all the decreases in.

Add stitches to body and rib as described above (Adjusting width at centre), and then half the extra stitches required to the number of stitches left on each shoulder after shaping is complete. This method is often best for cardigans and jackets, where the back neck needs to be a good fit.

Adding width at sides (fig. 3). The third option is to add the extra stitches under the arms. This can lead to complications with sleeves, but these can also be increased (see below: Adding width to set-in sleeves). This is particularly suitable for big chest measurements where shoulders/neck are not particularly large. For example, if your tension/gauge measures 26 sts (and 34 rows) to 4″ and you wish to add 5″ to the body of the sweater, you would calculate 26 × 5 ÷ 4 = 32½ stitches in all, i.e. 16 stitches to the back and 16 stitches to the front. So at each side of the back/front you would add 8 stitches (adjusting for stitch pattern and ribs (see Adjusting width at centre).

If the shape is a set-in sleeve, as fig. 3, take off a few of the extra stitches with the cast/bound off stitches at the beginning of the armhole shaping, and the remainder by working a few more decrease rows.

In our example, the original 4

cast/bound off stitches at each side have been increased to 8, and the decreasing rows given on the pattern would be repeated until the number of stitches remaining across the shoulders is reached; in this case, 4 extra decreases on each side.

Adding width to set-in sleeves (fig. 4). If you add width at the sides of a sweater, you will need to add only enough stitches to the sleeves to match the cast off stitches at each side at the beginning of top of sleeve shaping, i.e. in our example to increase them from 4 stitches to 8 on each side, a total increase of 8 stitches. On a classic sleeve, the shapings to increase the sleeve from cuff to underarm may need to be worked with fewer rows between them in order to gain the extra width without adding to the length.

Note: If a lot of stitches have been added to the front/back, with several more decrease rows than the pattern gives, consider also adding to the armhole depth of the front/back so that these extra stitches may be added at the centre of the sleeve, making larger the final number of stitches cast off at the *top* of the sleeves.

See page 70 for calculating the shape of set-in sleeves.

For more adjustment ideas, see the following page.

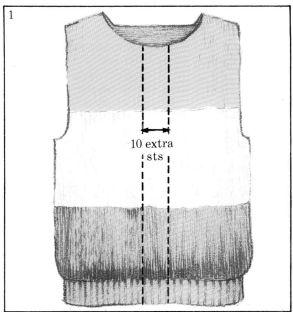

1. Adjusting width at centre.

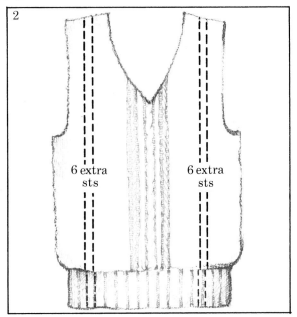

2. Adjusting width at shoulders.

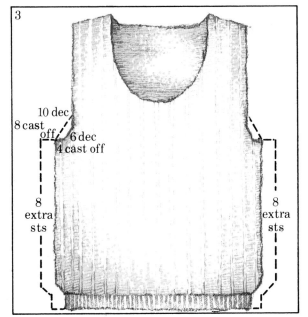

3. Adjusting width at sides.

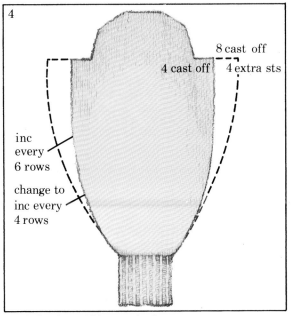

4. Adjusting width to set-in sleeves.

ALTERING EXISTING GARMENTS

For obvious reasons, this information applies particularly to children's garments. Suggestions on how to knit childrenswear so that it *can* be altered to fit later on are also given.

MAKING GARMENTS LARGER

Children's chest measurements vary by only a few inches whereas their sweater lengths vary proportionally much more. A sweater made to fit a 24" chest might easily measure 27" or 28" and not be too big, but in order to fit a larger child comfortably it might need to be 3" longer in body and sleeves. If the length can easily be altered, the sweater will give years of wear. Of course this is only really worth doing if the yarn is of good quality and has not been spoiled in washing.

Always use the same type of yarn, e.g. machine washable wool, of the same weight and preferably from the same manufacturer, to avoid future washing problems. It is not always necessary to use the same colour however.

Always try a tension/gauge square with the yarn you intend to use to make sure the tension matches the existing garment.

Wash the square if necessary before measuring. A record of the yarn and needles originally used will save you trouble.

When making a new sweater for a child, keep in mind that certain styles and methods (given below) are easier to alter than others.

Method 1: If you make a new garment by casting on the number of stitches required above the rib *first* (fig. 1), working the body; then picking up rib stitches and working rib downwards, you can unpick the cast/bound off edge of the ribbing and extend it downwards later on. Different coloured stripes may be added in the process.

Method 2: Choose a drop-shoulder style with no armhole shaping and little or no neck shaping (fig. 2a). When you make the sweater longer, unpick shoulder and armhole seams and cast/bound off edges; add on the extra length as in fig. 2b. Again a different colour can be quite effective, or a different stitch pattern; and with this shape, you can even increase over the extra sleeve rows to make the armholes deeper.

Method 3: If the sweater you are altering has both sleeve and neck shaping which are difficult to unpick, you can make it wider as shown in fig. 3.

Unpick the side and sleeve seams and add a knitted strip to each side. The strip can be straight, or shaped as shown to give maximum width where it is most required. If worked in a contrasting colour this can look most effective.

Method 4: If you have more of the same yarn as the garment but the garment has been washed several times, use one or more contrast stripes on the additions you make, or use a different textured stitch. This will hide the difference in colour.

The sweater in fig. 2a is altered in fig. 4 by unpicking the neck edge, shoulder seams, armhole seams and neck shaping, and adding the striped parts.

Fig. 5 shows fig. 2a again, this time made larger in both directions by adding sections in 2 contrasting colours and 2 different stitch patterns.

A cardigan or jacket may be made a little wider by adding wider bands: for instance, figs. 6 and 7 show a V-neck cardigan re-styled in this way, where the new bands are the same width as the lower welts/border.

MAKING GARMENTS SMALLER

To avoid unpicking work you can reduce the measurements as follows:

Reducing width. Either take in seams by 2 or 3 stitches at the sides (this method is not suitable for bulky yarns or stitch patterns) or, in desperate cases, cut the knitted pieces to shape.

To do this, mark the line you wish to cut with pins, following a straight line of stitches if possible, and use a sewing machine and matching thread to sew 2 or 3 lines of zig-zag stitch on top of each other just inside this line, before cutting along it (fig. 8). Do not cut the sewn stitches. Take an equal amount from each side of the piece.

Reducing length. One method is to bind with zig-zag stitches as described above (Reducing width). You will probably need to add a knitted border as in fig. 9, rather than pick up stitches to knit. Or you can bind the cut edge with fabric.

Grafting. This method of reducing length can be quite invisible and is really much the best way.

Cut through a stitch about 2″ from one side edge on the row *below* the lowest row of the part you wish to keep. Unpick the row, a few stitches at a time, slipping all the stitches without twisting them on to a fine knitting needle or threading them with a blunt needle on a length of thread.

Unravel the unwanted rows, and slip the stitches of the lower part you wish to keep on to another needle or thread.

Work on a flat surface with right sides facing you. See page 19 for grafting method. You can work equivalents for both K and P stitches. It is important to make the grafted stitches as nearly as possible the same tension as the rest of the knitting.

The position of the grafted line is important. Just above the lower welt/border is a good place so that if the line is a little tight or loose it will not show up very much.

If the main part is in a textured stitch which is difficult to copy in grafting, it can usually be grafted at this point in stocking stitch; but if there are increases across the top of the rib rows these will have to be worked into the grafted row by grafting 1 stitch from the lower edge to 2 stitches of the upper.

If the main part is in a 2-colour or fairisle pattern, reduce the length by a complete band of pattern.

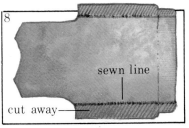

8 sewn line

cut away

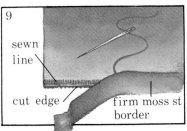

9 sewn line

cut edge

firm moss st border

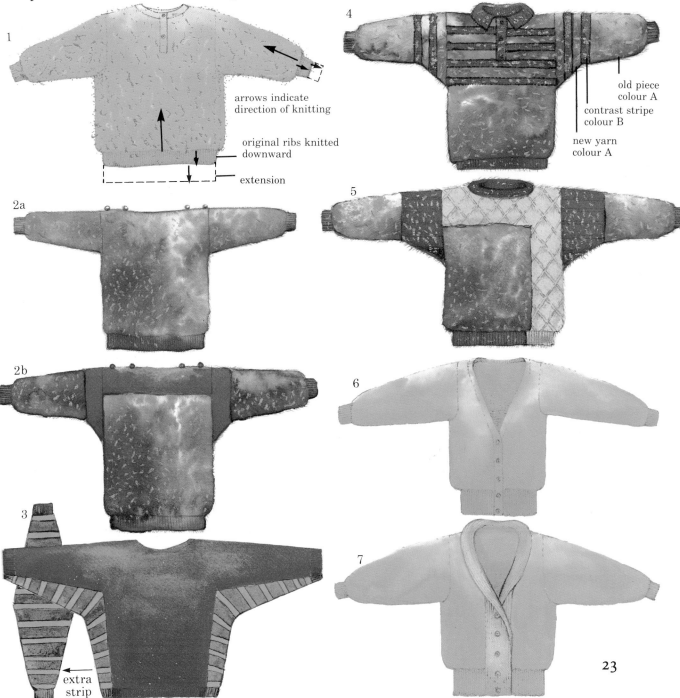

1 arrows indicate direction of knitting

original ribs knitted downward

extension

4 old piece colour A

contrast stripe colour B

new yarn colour A

2a

5

2b

6

3 extra strip

7

23

STITCH LIBRARY

The abbreviations used here are explained on the front endpapers.

BASIC STITCHES

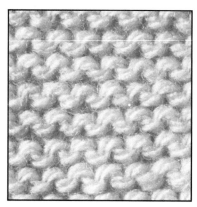

Garter

A reversible stitch which does not curl at the edges and has good elasticity. It was once used for garters, hence its name.
Worked over any number of sts.
row 1: K.
Rep. this row.
To work in the round, K the first and every alt round, P the 2nd and every alt round.

Stocking/stockinette

A stitch with good horizontal elasticity that was once used for stockings. A tendency to curl at the edges makes it unsuitable for edgings and borders, unless a hem is used. However, the fabric is smooth and flat. Most multi-colour knitting is worked in stocking/stockinette stitch.
row 1 (right side): K.
row 2: P.
Rep these 2 rows.
To work in the round, K every round.

Reverse stocking/stockinette

The reverse, or purl, side of st st forms a background to many cable and embossed patterns.

row 1 (right side): P.
row 2: K.
Rep these 2 rows.
To work in the round, P every round.

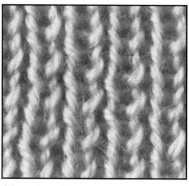

Single rib

Rib patterns have great sideways elasticity and are used most often where a garment needs to cling – for example, at waists and cuffs.
Worked over an even number of sts.
row 1: [K1, P1] to end.
row 2: [K1, P1] to end.
Rep these 2 rows.
To work in the round, [K1, P1] to end.
Rep this round.

Double rib

Worked over a multiple of 4 sts, plus 2 extra.
row 1: [K2, P2] to last 2 sts, K2.
row 2: [P2, K2] to last 2 sts, P2.

Rep these 2 rows.
To work in the round, cast on a multiple of 4 sts.
round 1: [K2, P2] to end.
Rep this round.

Irish moss.

Moss stitch

A tight, reversible fabric worked over an odd number of sts.
row 1: [K1, P1] to last st, K1.
Rep this row.
To work in the round, cast on an even number of sts.
round 1: [K1, P1] to end.
round 1: [P1, K1] to end.
Rep these 2 rounds.

Double moss

Worked over a multiple of 4 sts, plus 2 extra.
row 1: [K2, P2] to last 2 sts, K2.
row 2: [P2, K2] to last 2 sts, P2.
row 3: As 2nd.
row 4: As 1st.
Rep these 4 rows.
To work in the round, cast on a multiple of 4 sts.
rounds 1 and 2: [K2, P2] to end.
rounds 3 and 4: [P2, K2] to end.
Rep these 4 rounds.

Irish moss

Worked over a multiple of 2 sts.
row 1: [K1, P1] to end.
rows 2 and 4: Knit the K sts and purl the P sts as they face you.
row 3: [P1, K1] to end.

Corn stitch

This stitch should not be used for large areas of knitting because of its tendency to slant.
Worked over a multiple of 3 sts plus 1 extra.
row 1 (wrong side): P.
row 2: K1, [yrn/yo, K3, pass the 1st of these 3 sts over the following 2 sts] to end.
row 3: P.
row 4: [yrn/yo, K3, pass the 1st of these 3 sts over the following 2 sts] to last st, K1.
row 5: P.
row 6: K2, [yrn/yo, K3, pass the 1st of these 3 sts over the foll 2 sts] to last 2 sts, yrn/yo, K2tog.

Garter squares

Worked over a multiple of 6 sts.
rows 1, 3 and 5: Knit.
row 2 and every alt row: Purl.
rows 7, 9 and 11: [K3, P3] to end.
rows 13, 15 and 17: As row 1.
rows 19, 21 and 23: [P3, K3] to end.
row 24: As row 2.

Seed squares

Worked over a multiple of 10 sts plus 2 extra.
row 1: K1, [P1, K1, P1, K1, P6] to last st, K1.
row 2: K1, [K5, P1, K1, P1, K1, P1] to last st, K1.
rows 3, 5 and 7: As row 1.
rows 4, 6, and 8: As row 2.
row 9: K1, [P6, K1, P1, K1, P1] to last st, K1.
row 10: K1, [P1, K1, P1, K1, P1, K5] to last st, K1.
rows 11, 13 and 15: As row 9.
rows 12, 14 and 16: As row 10.

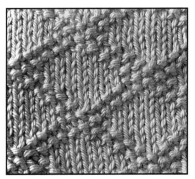

Diamond brocade

Worked over a multiple of 12 sts plus 1 extra.
row 1 (right side): K1, [P1, K9, P1, K1] to end.
row 2: K1, [P1, K1, P7, K1, P1, K1] to end.
row 3: K1, *P1, K1, P1, K5, [P1, K1] twice; repeat from * to end.
row 4: P1, *[P1, K1] twice, P3, K1, P1, K1, P2; repeat from * to end.
row 5: K1, *K2, [P1, K1] 3 times, P1, K3; repeat from * to end.
row 6: P1, *P3, [K1, P1] twice, K1, P4; repeat from * to end.
row 7: K1, *K4, P1, K1, P1, K5; repeat from * to end.
row 8: As row 6.
row 9: As row 5.
row 10: As row 4.
row 11: As row 3.
row 12: As row 2.

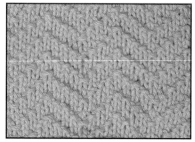

Raised chevron

Worked over a multiple of 8 sts.
row 1: [P1, K3] to end.
row 2: [K1, P5, K1, P1] to end.
row 3: [K2, P1, K3, P1, K1] to end.
row 4: [P2, K1, P1, K1, P3] to end.

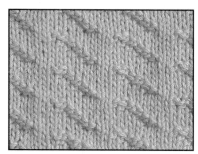

Diagonal

Worked over a multiple of 8 sts.
row 1: [K6, P2] to end.
row 2: [P1, K2, P5] to end.
row 3: [K4, P2, K2] to end.
row 4: [P3, K2, P3] to end.
row 5: [K2, P2, K4] to end.
row 6: Purl.

Step pattern

Worked over a multiple of 18 sts.
row 1: [K15, P3] to end.
row 2 and every alt row: K the K sts and P the P sts.
row 3: [K15, P3] to end.
rows 5 and 7: [K3, P15] to end.
rows 9 and 11: [K3, P3, K12] to end.
rows 13 and 15: [P6, K3, P9] to end.
rows 17 and 19: [K9, P3, K6] to end.
rows 21 and 23: [P12, K3, P3] to end.
row 24: As row 2.

Basketweave

Worked over a multiple of 8 sts, plus 4 extra.
row 1 (right side): K4, [P4, K4] to end.
row 2: P4, [K4, P4] to end.
rows 3 and 4: As rows 1 and 2.
rows 5 and 7: As row 2.
rows 6 and 8: As row 1.

Irish moss diamond

Worked over a multiple of 14 sts.
row 1: *[P1, K1] 4 times, K6; repeat from * to end.
row 2 and every alt row: K the K sts and P the P sts as they face you.
row 3: *[K1, P1] 3 times, K4, P1, K3; repeat from * to end.
row 5: [K2, P1, K1, P1, K4, P1, K1, P1, K2] to end.
row 7: *K3, P1, K4, [P1, K1] 3 times; repeat from * to end.
row 9: *K6, [K1, P1] 4 times; repeat from * to end.
row 11: As row 7.
row 13: As row 5.
row 15: As row 3.
row 16: As row 2.

EYELET
AND LACE

Filigree

Worked over a multiple of 14 sts plus 2 extra.
row 1: P1, [P2, K2tog, K3, yrn/yo, K1, yrn/yo, K3, skpo, P1]; repeat to last st, P1.
row 2 and every alt row: K the K sts and P the P sts and yrn/yo sts, as they face you.
row 3: P1, [P2, K2tog, K2, yrn/yo, K3, yrn/yo, K2, skpo, P1]; repeat to last st, P1.
row 5: P1, [P2, K2tog, K1, yrn/yo, K5, yrn/yo, K1, skpo, P1]; repeat to last st, P1.
row 7: P1, [P2, K2tog, yrn/yo, K7, yrn/yo, skpo, P1]; repeat to last st, P1.
row 9: P1, [K1, yrn/yo, K3, skpo, P3, K2tog, K3, yrn/yo]; repeat to last st, P1.
row 11: P1, [K2, yrn/yo, K2, skpo, P3, K2tog, K2, yrn/yo, K1]; repeat to last st, P1.
row 13: P1, [K3, yrn/yo, K1, skpo, P3, K2tog, K1, yrn/yo, K2]; repeat to last st, P1.
row 15: P1, [K4, yrn/yo, skpo, P3, K2tog, yrn/yo, K3], repeat to last st, P1.
row 16: As row 2.

Eyelet pattern

Worked over a multiple of 8 sts, plus 7 extra.
row 1 and every alt row (wrong side): Purl.
row 2: Knit.
row 4: K2, yrn/yo, sl 1, k2tog, psso, yrn/yo, [K5, yrn/yo, sl 1, K2tog, psso, yrn/yo]; repeat to last 2 sts, K2.
row 6: K3, yrn/yo, skpo, [K6, yrn/yo, skpo]; repeat to last 2 sts, K2.
row 8: Knit.
row 10: K1, [K5, yrn/yo, sl 1, K2tog, psso, yrn/yo]; repeat to last 6 sts, K6.
row 12: K7, [yrn/yo, skpo, K6] to end.

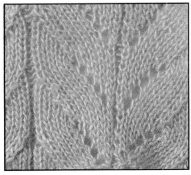

Spiral lace

Worked over a multiple of 25 sts plus 2 extra.

Special abbreviation

SSK = slip next 2 sts singly to right hand needle knitwise, insert tip of left needle through front loop of both sts and knit together.

row 1: [P2, K4, K2tog, K4, yrn/yo, K1 tbl, P1, K1 tbl, yrn/yo, K4, SSK, K4]; repeat to last 2 sts, P2.

row 2 and every alt row: K2, [P11, K1, P11, K2]; repeat to end.

row 3: [P2, K3, K2tog, K4, yrn/yo, K1, K1 tbl, P1, K1 tbl, K1, yrn/yo, K4, SSK, K3]; repeat to last 2 sts, P2.

row 5: [P2, K2, K2tog, K4, yrn/yo, K2, K1 tbl, P1, K1 tbl, K2, yrn/yo, K4, SSK, K2]; repeat to last 2 sts, P2.

row 7: [P2, K1, K2tog, K4, yrn/yo, K3, K1 tbl, P1, K1 tbl, K3, yrn/yo, K4, SSK, K1]; repeat to last 2 sts, P2.

row 9: [P2, K2tog, K4, yrn/yo, K4, K1 tbl, P1, K1 tbl, K4, yrn/yo, K4, SSK]; repeat to last 2 sts, P2.

row 10: As row 2.

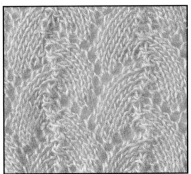

Shell lace

Worked over a multiple of 11 sts plus 1. (Worked over a minimum of 23 sts.)

row 1: K2tog, [K5, yrn/yo, K1, yrn/yo, K2, sl 1, K2tog, psso]; repeat to last 10 sts, K5, yrn/yo, K1, yrn/yo, K2, K2tog tbl.

row 2 and every alt row: Purl.

row 3: K2tog, [K4, yrn/yo, K3,

yrn/yo, K1, sl 1, K2tog, psso]; to last 10 sts, K4, yrn/yo, K3, yrn/yo, K1, K2tog tbl.

row 5: K2tog, [K3, yrn/yo, K5, yrn/yo, sl 1, K2tog, psso]; to last 10 sts, K3, yrn/yo, K5, yrn/yo, K2tog tbl.

row 7: K2tog, [K2, yrn/yo, K1, yrn/yo, K5, sl 1, K2tog, psso]; repeat to last 10 sts, K2, yrn/yo, K1, yrn/yo, K5, K2tog tbl.

row 9: K2 tog, [K1, yrn/yo, K3, yrn/yo, K4, sl 1, K2tog, psso]; repeat to last 10 sts, K1, yrn/yo, K3, yrn/yo, K4, K2tog tbl.

row 11: K2tog, [yrn/yo, K5, yrn/yo, K3, sl 1, K2tog, psso]; repeat to last 10 sts, yrn/yo, K5, yrn/yo, K3, K2tog tbl.

row 12: as row 2.

Feather and fan

Worked over a multiple of 13 sts.

row 1: *K4, [yrn/yo, K1] 5 times, yrn/yo, K4; repeat from * to end.

row 2: Purl.

row 3: *[P2tog] 3 times, P7, [P2tog] 3 times; repeat from * to end.

rows 4 and 5: Knit.

row 6: Purl.

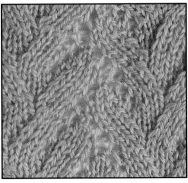

Tree lattice

Worked over a multiple of 13 sts plus 2.

row 1: K1, [K2, skpo, K4, K2tog, K2, yrn/yo, K1, yrn/yo]; repeat to last st, K1.

row 2 and every alt row: Purl.

row 3: K1, [yrn/yo, K2, skpo, K2, K2tog, K2, yrn/yo, K3]; repeat to

last st, K1.

row 5: K1, [K1, yrn/yo, K2, skpo, K2tog, K2, yrn/yo, K4]; repeat to last st, K1.

row 7: K1, [yrn/yo, K1, yrn/yo, K2, skpo, K4, K2tog, K2]; repeat to last st, K1.

row 9: K1, [K3, yrn/yo, K2, skpo, K2, K2tog, K2, yrn/yo]; repeat to last st, K1.

row 11: K1, [K4, yrn/yo, K2, skpo, K2tog, K2, yrn/yo, K1]; repeat to last st, K1.

row 12: As row 2.

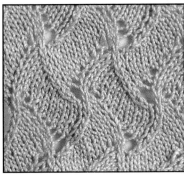

Scroll

Worked over a multiple of 10 sts plus 2.

row 1: K1, [yrn/yo, K8, K2tog]; repeat to last st, K1.

row 2: P1, [P2tog, P7, yrn/yo, P1]; repeat to last st, P1.

row 3: K1, [K2, yrn/yo, K6, K2tog]; repeat to last st, K1.

row 4: P1, [P2tog, P5, yrn/yo, P3]; repeat to last st, P1.

row 5: K1, [K4, yrn/yo, K4, K2tog]; repeat to last st, K1.

row 6: P1, [P2tog, P3, yrn/yo, P5]; repeat to last st, P1.

row 7: K1, [K6, yrn/yo, K2, K2tog]; repeat to last st, K1.

row 8: P1, [P2tog, P1, yrn/yo, P7]; repeat to last st, P1.

row 9: K1, [K8, yrn/yo, K2tog]; repeat to last st, K1.

row 10: P1, [yrn/yo, P8, P2tog tbl]; repeat to last st, P1.

row 11: K1, [skpo, K7, yrn/yo, K1]; repeat to last st, K1.

row 12: P1, [P2, yrn/yo, P6, P2tog tbl]; repeat to last st, P1.

row 13: K1, [skpo, K5, yrn/yo, K3]; repeat to last st, K1.

row 14: P1, [P4, yrn/yo, P4, P2tog tbl]; repeat to last st, P1.

row 15: K1, [skpo, K3, yrn/yo, K5]; repeat to last st, K1.

row 16: P1, [P6, yrn/yo, P2, P2tog tbl]; repeat to last st, P1.

row 17: K1, [skpo, K1, yrn/yo, K7]; repeat to last st, K1.

row 18: P1, [P8, yrn/yo, P2tog tbl]; repeat to last st, P1.

CABLE, BOBBLE AND ARAN

The following are special abbreviations used in the cable, bobble and aran patterns. (For instructions on using cable needles, see page 17.)

C6F = slip next 3 sts to cable needle and hold at front, K3, then K3 from cable needle.

C6B = slip next 3 sts to cable needle and hold at back, K3 then K3 from cable needle.

C5B = slip next 2 sts to cable needle and hold at back, K3, then P2 from cable needle.

C5F = slip next 3 sts to cable needle and hold at front, P2, then K3 from cable needle.

MB = make bobble thus, (K1, yrn/yo, K1, yrn/yo, K1) all into next st, turn, P5, turn, K5, turn, P2tog, P1, P2tog, turn sl 1, K2tog, psso.

Shadow Cable

Worked over a multiple of 12 sts plus 2 extra.
row 1: Knit.
row 2 and every alt row: Purl.
row 3: K1, [C6F, K6]; repeat to last st, K1.

row 5: Knit.
row 7: K1, [K6, C6B]; repeat to last st, K1.
row 8: Purl.

Knot stitch

Worked over a multiple of 8 sts plus 5 extra.
rows 1, 3 and 5: Knit.
rows 2, 4 and 6: Purl.
row 7: K5, *[P3tog, K3tog, P3tog] into next 3 sts, K5; repeat from * to end.
rows 8, 10, 12 and 14: Purl.
rows 9, 11 and 13: Knit.
row 15: K1, *[P3tog, K3tog, P3tog] into next 3 sts, K5; repeat from * to last st, K1.
row 16: Purl.

Field of wheat

Worked over 11 sts, plus 2 extra. (Stitches will be made in one row and lost in another.)
row 1 (right side): K1, [K5, yrn/yo, K1, yrn/yo, K3, K2tog] repeat to last st, K1.
rows 2, 4, 6 and 8: P1, [P2tog, P10] repeat to last st, P1.
row 3: K1, [K6, yrn/yo, K1, yrn/yo, K2, K2tog] repeat to last st, K1.
row 5: K1, *K7, [yrn/yo, K1] twice, K2tog; repeat from * to last st, K1.
row 7: K1, [K8, yrn/yo, K1, yrn/yo, K2tog] repeat to last st, K1.
row 9: K1, [skpo, K4, yrn/yo, K1, yrn/yo, K2, MB, K1] repeat to last st, K1.

row 10: P1, [P1, P1 tbl, P8, P2tog, tbl] repeat to last st, P1.
row 11: K1, [skpo, K3, yrn/yo, K1, yrn/yo, K5] repeat to last st, K1.
rows 12, 14, 16 and 18: P1, [P10, P2tog tbl] repeat to last st, P1.
row 13: K1, [sklpo, K3, yrn/yo, K1, yrn/yo, K5] repeat to last st, K1.
row 15: K1, *skpo, [K1, yrn/yo] twice, K7; repeat from * to last st, K1.
row 17: K1, [skpo, yrn/yo, K1, yrn/yo, K8] repeat to last st, K1.
row 19: K1, [K1, MB, K2, yrn/yo, K1, yrn/yo, K4, K2tog] repeat to last st, K1.
row 20: P1, [P2tog, P8, P1 tbl, P1] repeat to last st, P1.

Chevron cable

Worked over a multiple of 12 sts plus 2 extra.
row 1 and every alt row (wrong side): Purl.
row 2: K1, [C6B, C6F] to last st, K1.
rows 4, 6 and 8: Knit.

Twisted cable

Worked over a multiple of 9 sts plus 3 extra.

rows 1 and 3: [P3, K6]; repeat to last 3 sts, P3.
rows 2 and 4: [K3, P6]; repeat to last 3 sts, K3.
row 5: [P3, C6B]; repeat to last 3 sts, P3.
row 6: [K3, P6]; repeat to last 3 sts, K3.

Simple bobbles

Worked over a multiple of 6 sts plus 5 extra.

rows 1 and 3 (right side): Knit.
row 2 and every alt row: Purl.
row 5: K5, [MB, K5] to end.
rows 7 and 9: Knit.
row 11: K2, [MB, K5] repeat to last 3 sts, K3.
row 12: As row 2.

Bramble stitch

Worked over a multiple of 4 sts.
row 1 (wrong side): K2, *[K1, P1, K1] into next st, P3tog; repeat from * to last 2 sts, K2.
row 2: Purl.
row 3: K2, *P3tog, [K1, P1, K1] into next st; repeat from * to last 2 sts, K2.
row 4: As row 2.

Plaited cable

Worked over 29 sts.
row 1: K1, P1, K3, [P4, K6] twice, P3, K1.
row 2 and every alt row: K the K sts and P the P sts as they face you.
row 3: K1, P1, K3, [P4, C6F] twice, P3, K1.

Row 5: K1, P1, [C5F, C5B] twice, C5F, P1, K1.
row 7: K1, P3, [C6B, P4] twice, K3, P1, K1.
row 9: K1, P1, [C5B, C5F] twice, C5B, P1, K1.
row 10: As row 2.
Rep from row 3.

Lattice pattern

Special abbreviations
C4B = cable 4 back, slip 2 sts to cable needle and hold at back, K2, then K2 from cable needle.
Cr4B = slip 2 sts to cable needle and hold at back, K2, then P2 from cable needle.
C4F = slip 2 sts to cable needle and hold at front, K2, then K2 from cable needle.
Cr4F = slip 2 sts to cable needle and hold at front, P2, then K2 from cable needle.

Worked over a multiple of 6 sts.
row 1: [K4, P2] to end.
row 2 and every alt row: K the K sts and P the P sts as they face you.
row 3: [C4B, P2] to end.
row 5: P2, [K2, Cr4B]; repeat to last 4 sts, K4.
row 7: [P2, C4F] to end.
row 9: K4, [Cr4F, K2]; repeat to last 2 sts, P2.
row 10: As row 2.
Repeat from row 3.

COLOUR PATTERNS

Spot check

Worked over a multiple of 6 sts plus 5.

row 1: using main colour, knit.
row 2: Purl.
row 3: using contrast, K1, [sl 3, K3]; repeat to last 4 sts, sl 3, K1.
row 4: P2, [sl 1P, P5]; repeat to last 3 sts, sl 1P, P2.
row 5: Knit.
row 6: Purl.
row 7: using main colour, K4, [sl 3, K3]; repeat to last st, K1.
row 8: P5, [sl 1P, P5]; repeat to end.

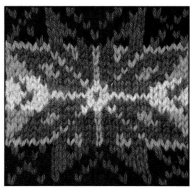

Fairisle snowflake

Worked over a multiple of 30 sts, plus one, using 6 colours (A, B, C, D, E, F).
Cast on in A. Join in D.
row 1 (right side): [K1D, 2A, 1D, 3A, 1D, 1A, 1D, 2A, 1D, 5A, 1D, 2A, 1D, 1A, 1D, 3A, 1D, 2A]; repeat to last st, K1D.
row 2: P1D, [P1D, 2A, 1D, 1A, 1D, 2A, 2D, 2A, 1D, 3A, 1D, 2A, 2D, 2A, 1D, 1A, 1D, 2A, 2D] to end.
This sets the position of pattern.
Beg with 3rd row cont in pattern from chart, repeat the 25 rows, working a purl row using A between repeats.

Multi-colour stripes

Worked over a multiple of 4 sts, plus 3 and using 4 colours (A, B, C, D).

row 1 (Wrong side): using A, Purl.
row 2: using B, K2, [sl 1 with yarn back, K1]; repeat to last st, K1.
row 3: using B, P2, [sl 1 with yarn front, P1]; repeat to last st, P1.
row 4: Using C, K1, [sl 1 with yarn back, K1] to end.
row 5: using C, Purl.
row 6: using D, K1, [sl 1 with yarn back, K3]; repeat to last 2 sts, sl 1 with yarn back, K1.
row 7: using D, P1, [sl 1 with yarn forward, P3]; repeat to last 2 sts, sl 1 with yarn forward, P1.
row 8: using B, K2, [sl 3 with yarn back, K1]; repeat to last st, K1.
row 9: using B, [P3, sl 1 with yarn forward]; repeat to last 3 sts, P3.
row 10: using A, K1, [sl 1 with yarn back, K3]; repeat to last 2 sts, sl 1 with yarn forward, K1.

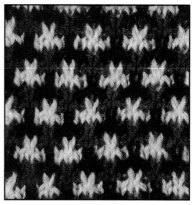

Rabbit pattern

Worked over a multiple of 4 sts plus 2 and using 3 colours (A, B, C). On rows 4 and 6 yarn is brought forward and taken back *between* needles, *without* making extra sts.

row 1: using A, Knit.
row 2: using A, Purl.
row 3: using B, K1, [K3, sl 1]; repeat to last st, K1.
row 4: using B, P1, [yarn forward, sl 1, yarn back, P3]; repeat to last st, P1.
row 5: using C, K2, [sl 1, K3]; repeat to last 4 sts, sl 1, K3.
row 6: using C, P3, [yarn forward, sl 1, yarn back, P3]; repeat to last 3 sts, sl 1, P2.
rows 7 and 8: using A, as rows 3 and 4.
rows 9 and 10: using B, as rows 5 and 6.
rows 11 and 12: using C, as rows 3 and 4.

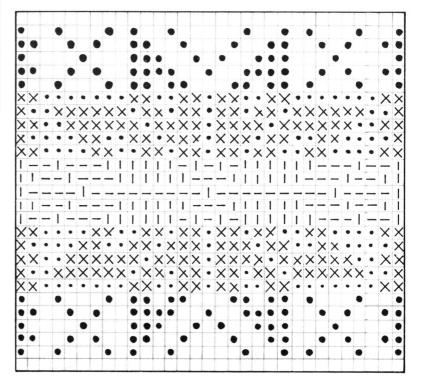

rows 13 and 14: using A, as rows 5 and 6.
Repeat from row 3.

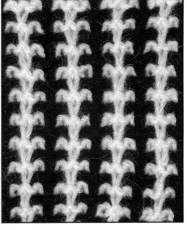

Three colour pattern

Worked over a multiple of 3 sts, plus 1 and using 3 colours (A, B, C).
row 1 (wrong side): using A, Knit.
row 2: using B, K3, [sl 1 with yarn back, K2]; repeat to last st, K1.
row 3: using B, K3, [sl 1 with yarn forward, K2]; repeat to last st, K1.
row 4: using C, [K2, sl 1 with yarn back]; repeat to last st, K1.
row 5: using C, K1, [sl 1 with yarn forward, K2] to end.
row 6: using A, K1, [sl 1 with yarn back, K2] to end.
row 7: using A, [K2, sl 1 with yarn forward]; repeat to last st, K1.
Repeat rows 2 to 7.

Tweed

Worked over an uneven number of sts, using 2 colours (A, B).
row 1: using A, Purl.
row 2: using B, K1, [sl 1, K1] to end.
row 3: using B, Purl.
row 4: using A, K1, [sl 1, K1] to end.
row 5: using A, Purl.
row 6: using B, [sl 1, K1]; repeat to last st, K1.
row 7: using B, Purl.
row 8: using A, K2, [sl 1, K1]; repeat to last st, K1.
row 9: using A, Purl.
Repeat rows 2 to 9.

Two-colour tweed

Worked over a multiple of 4 sts plus 3 extra.
Cast on in contrast.
row 1 (wrong side): using contrast, Knit.
row 2: using main colour, K3, [sl 1 with yarn at back, K3] to end.
row 3: using main colour, K3, [sl 1 with yarn at front, K3] to end.
row 4: using contrast, K1, [sl 1 with yarn at back, K3]; repeat to last 2 sts, sl 1 with yarn at back, K1.
row 5: using contrast, K1, [sl 1 with yarn at front, K3]; repeat to last 2 sts, sl 1 with yarn at front, K1.
Repeat rows 2 to 5.

Shetland diamond

Worked over a multiple of 12 sts, plus one, using 3 colours (A, B, C).
Cast on in A. Join in B.
row 1 (right side): [K1A, 4B, 1A, 1B, 1A, 4B]; repeat to last st, K1A.
row 2: P1A, *P1A, 2B, [1A, 1B] twice, 1A, 2B, 2A; repeat from * to end.
This sets the position of pattern.
Beg with 3rd row cont in pattern from chart, rep 12 rows as required. To complete pattern work row 1 again.

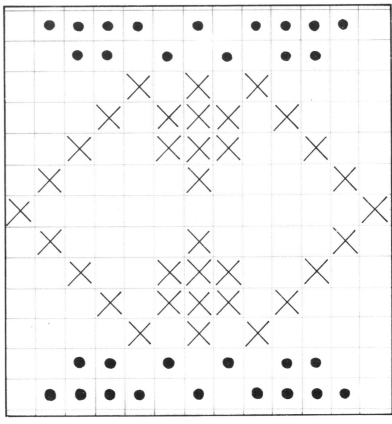

31

THE BASIC SHAPES

A knitted square makes a pocket, or a cushion cover. Keep on knitting and it becomes a scarf. Knit four rectangles and sew them together and you have a drop-shoulder sweater, or, knit them as one piece and it's a T shape, shown opposite. All of this serves to emphasize the fact that, in terms of shape, knitting is primarily about rectangles: it is built up in linear rows and, even for clothing, involves mainly rectangular shapes: bodice fronts and backs, sleeves, collars, cuffs. It is by refining these overall rectangular outlines, honing each one of them down to fit more and more precisely body shape, that tailored knitwear patterns are developed – beautifully moulded set-in or raglan sleeves, finely-tapered bodices and curving necklines.

SWEATERS

Sweaters are probably the most popular of all the current usages of knitting, and over the years a number of established categories of sweater have evolved, each of them based on a specific sleeve style. The sweaters illustrated in this chapter are divided into these categories: T shape, drop shoulder, batwing, set-in sleeve and raglan, and they are accompanied by patterns with step-by-step instructions which begin on page 99. These will enable each of the sweaters to be copied exactly as it appears, but the patterns are arranged and organized in such a way that they can also be used as templates from which to create individual variations, while keeping a particular type of sleeve. Before beginning either to knit one of the patterns or to adapt it, it is important to read the introduction to the pattern section (page 99), and also Adapting pattern measurements, page 20.

Some readers may wish to develop their confidence by going through every stage: first, following step-by-step instructions, then adapting one of the patterns using a different yarn and adjusting the tension/gauge accordingly – and, finally, exchanging one neckline for another, widening or narrowing the bodice or sleeve width, and adding personal finishing details. More experienced knitters, on the other hand, may find some of the patterns suited to their needs as they appear, and others an excellent basis for reinterpretation and design.

INSPIRATION

Inspiration is the key to all innovation and there is a wealth of source material if we will use our eyes: fabrics exhibited in museums and in pictures, clothing and knitwear on sale in shops, magazines. Remember nothing is wrong or right so long as it is pleasing to the eye and touch. To help facilitate new design ideas and adaptations, however, each of the sections in this chapter is followed by a display of colourful fashion sketches which can be used either to provide a stimulus for adapting the patterns illustrated, or to inspire the knitter's own ideas about design when developing new patterns of one's own.

T SHAPE

Sailor Stripes

T shapes can be knitted in one piece then folded in two to make a T, or they can be knitted in two pieces and joined at the shoulders, as shown overleaf. The point is that there is no separate sleeve to be attached, and that is what gives this shape its appealing simplicity.

The teenager's sweater is in stocking/stockinette stitch with garter stitch trim; the little girl's, suitable for beginners – garter stitch throughout. Patterns on pages 100–101.

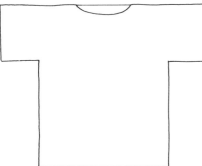

Two Stitches

Left: the textural effect of simple stitches is well-illustrated in this yellow cotton sweater knitted half in stocking/stockinette stitch and half in reverse stocking/stockinette stitch. Sleeves are tapered and the neckline gently scooped. Pattern on page 101.

Ribbon Top

Below: silky viscose ribbon yarn in steel grey. Smart and very simple, knitted in stocking/stockinette stitch with small sleeves and a slash neck-line. Choice of yarn dictates the mood entirely: summer, winter, day or evening wear. Pattern on page 102.

Below: sleeve depth is what
counts here. Easy to knit and
simple to design: choice of yarn
and stitch sets the mood.

Left: two colours changes the appearance
of the Two Stitches sweater shown on page
34. The same pattern is adapted on the
right with wide collar and band of fairisle
snowflakes (see Stitch Library). Aran
weight wool will approximate the same
tension/gauge as pattern's.

Left: pullover knitted in cable,
which in T shape runs horizontally
round the sleeve. Base on Sailor
Stripes (page 33), substituting rib
welts and cuffs, and a round neck
(page 80), but remember that stitch
multiples have to be worked out
before casting on.

Below: patchwork
squares. Choose your own
colour combination or stick
to one colour and use different
textures such as aran stitch patterns,
keeping tension/gauge constant.

DROP SHOULDER

Because of its simple unshaped sleeve head, the drop shoulder is one of the easiest and most popular pattern styles to design or make. Since it is designed normally to fit loosely and has more 'ease' than many other styles, it lends itself to sporty looks. A variety of yarns are suitable: wool especially, but also cottons and synthetics since a loose fit can be highly desirable in summer knitwear. This shape makes a good background too for large or abstract motifs knitted in stocking/stockinette stitch, or alternatively for innovative stitch patterns such as the cable or two-colour patterns in the Stitch Library.

Round or slash necklines seem to suit this style best – and they help to keep its loose and often bulky shape in position. Because the shoulder of the garment forms a part of the sleeve, the sleeve itself is always proportionately shorter. Sleeveless, the drop shoulder forms a natural 'cap' over the upper arm.

A variation of the drop shoulder is the half drop which is illustrated on page 67. In this style the sleeves are slightly recessed into the bodice which makes a more closely fitting garment possible. They suggest too the development of the more carefully contoured set-in sleeve described further on.

Mohair cowl

Opposite: brilliant purple edged in gold – a bold and stunning effect which shows how colour can transform even the simplest design, knitted here in stocking-stockinette stitch. The sweater has a round neckline, tapered sleeves and ribbed edging. The cowl is made separately. *Pattern on page 103.*

Adam's Rib

Right: the same shape exactly as the purple mohair on the previous page, but knitted here in broken rib stitch using a tweed double knitting/ worsted yarn. Pattern on page 105.

Swirling leaves

Another extremely simple shape which makes an inviting palette for motifs picked out in vivid colours. Yarn is used double for a chunky effect, and therefore it is quick to knit. The motifs are charted stitch-by-stitch on a graph, but you could design your own decoration following instructions in the Colour and Texture chapter. Pattern on page 107.

Floppy shirt

Far right: taupe cotton contributes a casual elegance to the drop shoulder shape. Inset pocket and a button front neckline. Or it could be lengthened to make a shirtwaist dress, remeasuring and using information on calculating yarns. Pattern on page 106.

Duffel coat: an elongated drop shoulder cardigan. Choose a chunky/bulky yarn and firm stitch such as Irish moss or seed stitch.

Right: lace feminizes the casual drop shoulder style. Scooped neck (page 81) and tree lattice pattern (page 27). Can be based on Floppy Shirt, tightening welt and cuffs and omitting button front.

Below: Mohair Cowl (page 39) could be the template decorated with geometric blocks worked in fairisle (page 95); collar, tapered sleeve.

Right: drop shoulder style extended to dress length and decorated with two cables. Use chunky/bulky wool and base on Swirling Leaves pattern, allowing a few extra stitches to be taken up in cabling; change collar to round neck (page 80).

Above: cowl sweater on page 39 shown in a different yarn. Suggest heavy weight cotton or chunky/bulky wool.

Left: silky sleeveless drop shoulder. See designing V necks on page 78.

BATWING

The original inspiration for batwing sleeves is evident in its name. The flowing excess of a soft, knitted fabric underarm is luxuriant, if in humans sometimes a little impractical: unlike the bat we cannot fold it away properly, so it can be difficult to wear under coats and jackets. For this reason, the batwing very often is at its best as an over garment, or as evening wear when a shawl or stole may comfortably replace a coat.

Soft or supple yarns are preferable, but this includes the more dramatic yarns suitable for evening wear such as shiny viscose mixtures, also bead or sequin trim, described on page 98. The batwing shape is essentially a rather lavish variation on the T shape, and like it can be knitted either in one or two pieces.

A permutation of the batwing is the dolman sleeve, described on page 69. Derived from Turkish robe styles, its difference from batwing is one of degree: there is less fullness in the underarm, making the dolman somewhere between T shape and batwing. A summer version of dolman is the short sleeve illustrated in the sketch below.

Cable motif

Opposite: to fully appreciate the symmetry of this shape it is necessary to look at the pattern diagram. The garment is knitted in one piece, a huge diamond with cables running like an engraved decoration from end to end. Pattern on page 110.

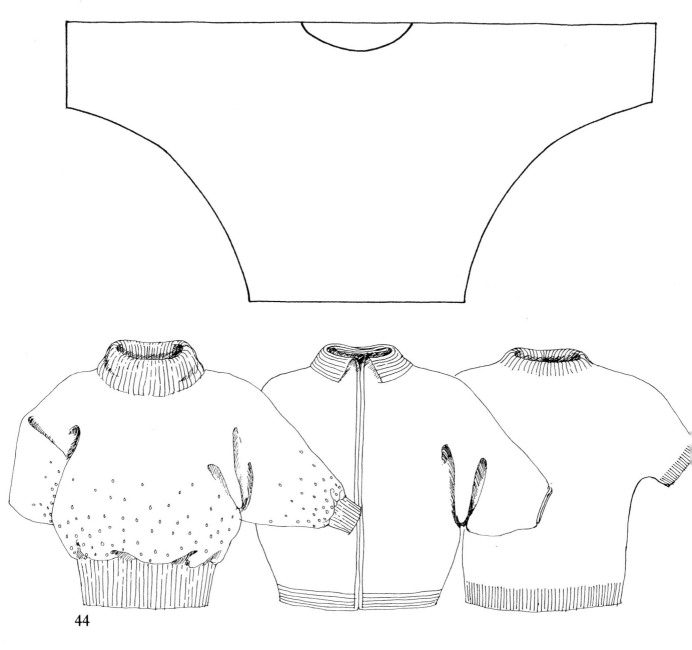

Snow white

*A combination of twist rib and diamond pattern in soft aran weight yarn
with zip front. This is batwing at its best since as an outer garment the deep
sleeves are an asset rather than a hindrance. The pattern is one for more
confident knitters, and novices may prefer to keep the shape but work out the
tension/gauge required to knit it in a more basic stitch or stitch combination.
Pattern illustrated on page 111.*

Left: pattern of pullover needs a
specially soft wool such as angora.
Measurements can be taken from
Cable Motif, adding V neck (page
78) and a different stitch pattern.

Boat neck grey batwing and
version below with crew neck
both in stocking/stockinette stitch
show how much yarn type and
choice of colour matter.

Left: plunging V neck,
wide ribbed welt. A
wonderful design for
evening wear: jet black or
a luxurious yarn – silk,
angora, or a touch of
lurex?

Simple cardigan buttoning at welt. Cable Motif style could be used as base and adapted to cardigan as described on page 86. Knit from cuffs inward to change appearance of stitch.

SET-IN SLEEVES

This classic sweater shape was borrowed from dressmaking techniques and adapted to the knitting craft in order to make it possible for garments to fit body contours more precisely. Since the curve of the sleeve head has to be calculated to fit the recessed curve of the armhole, it is one of the more complex forms of patternmaking in knitwear as well as dressmaking. Information on how to make the necessary calculations is given in the Tailoring chapter, but the patterns can be used as guides, keeping the sleeve while varying other aspects of the patterns – yarn, stitch, length of sleeve and so on.

In set-in sleeve styles the 'ease' allowance is very often less than it is in other styles, although bloused shapes are also popular. Set-in sleeves fit beautifully under slim-line jackets and coats, although the armhole should never be very tight, particularly with heavier yarns. Sleeves can be any length, or sleeveless. The puff sleeve, a highly feminine variant, exhibits a luxurious softness when supple yarn is used. And because the sleeve head is gathered, it is marginally easier to adapt and to design than is the fitted shape.

Sunburst

Opposite: nostalgic bobble and lace stitch pattern, puff sleeves and short, slightly bloused bodice. Entirely feminine in expression, but as the photograph shows, what you wear it with makes a big difference to the overall effect. Pattern on page 113.

Fairisle cardigan

Traditionally, fairisle is knitted in wool; here pastel colours knitted in pure mercerized cotton confer a summer interpretation. But the cardigan could also be knitted in wool, or in one colour, or in a textured stitch pattern such as cable. It is essentially a matter of the right tension/gauge and of estimating the yarn requirements correctly (both are described elsewhere in this book). Pattern on page 115.

Man's Fairisle

V neck pullover, probably the most popular of all masculine sweater styles. It can be knitted as shown in shetland type wool, or used as a template for any number of yarns and stitch patterns. Pattern on page 117.

Scottie sweater

Knitted in DK/worsted yarn in stocking/stockinette stitch, the back of the sweater has the same zig-zag stripe and scottie dog motif as on the front. Use this pattern for a basic plain version too – instructions fit up to 34 inch chest. Pattern on page 118.

Three versions of the classic pullover. Both the diamond pattern and the repeating cherry motif must be worked out on a graph (see page 95 for instructions). The red pullover relies on pockets (page 88) hidden in a wide welt and soft fluffy yarn for its originality.

Left: comfortable summer style. Sleeveless with button front (page 84), knitted in cotton.

Puffed sleeve cardigan version of Sunburst jumper. Here sleeves are made even wider (above cuff) and gathered more at the top. Knitted in stocking/stockinette stitch. Instructions for adapting pullovers to cardigans appear on page 86.

Far right: spiral lace pattern from Stitch Library knitted with lightweight yarn – silky rayon or fine fluffy type – with peplum (page 65) and collar (page 83).

RAGLAN

The distinguishing feature of the raglan style is that the sleeve head forms both the shoulder and a part of the sweater neckline. The raglan gets its name from Lord Raglan, who wore an overcoat of this shape in the Crimean war. Cardigans have a similar derivation, being named after Lord Raglan's colleague, Lord Cardigan, who led the disastrous charge of the light brigade in the same war.

Like the set-in sleeve, the raglan is designed to fit closely the contours of the body, but the raglan style tends to be less formal and more comfortable and relaxed. Not surprisingly it is a very popular sleeve for cardigans, and sporty yarns such as shetland. Raglans look well on any size person. Quite often the seam lines joining sleeves and bodice are embellished by decorative decreasing techniques, while, sleeveless, the resulting bare shouldered halter effect can be most attractive.

Plotting a raglan pattern is described elsewhere in this book, but it is easy to use the basic outline given in these patterns and adapt them to personal tastes, keeping sleeves and armholes constant.

Opposite: striking mohair coat knitted using the intarsia method in stocking/stockinette stitch with blocks of garter stitch. Embroidered chain stitch makes the dark vertical lines. Pattern on page 121.

Christmas

Left: a blend of mohair and silky viscose, wide neck and button shoulder fastening. For day or night. Pattern on page 123.

His and Hers

V-neck pullover and cardigan made from the same basic pattern and using the same yarn and needle sizes. Pattern, page 124.

Raglan coat: one-colour adaptation of the mohair coat on page 57 using chunky/bulky wool. Could be knitted in shadow cable (see Stitch Library).

Left: raglan V neck shown on page 59, knitted in twisted cable and bramble stitch patterns from the Stitch Library. A DK/worsted or aran weight wool is recommended.

Classic raglan cardigan tinged with 1940s nostalgia. 4 ply (fingering) or DK/worsted wool.

Below: baggy raglan should be knitted in a soft pliable yarn such as cotton chainette.

TAILORING

Like all clothing, knitwear requires tailoring: there are different bodice shapes, sleeve shapes, necklines and collars, pockets, etc.; and by studying the principles governing each of these features, you can decide upon and make your own combinations.

Before tackling pattern adaptation or new designs however, a sound working knowledge of three things is vitally important. They are, measuring and 'ease' (chapter 1), correct tension/gauge (page 12), and increasing and decreasing stitches (pages 14 and 15). None of these are the least bit complicated; they are basic to knitting technique as well as the tools by which design is added to the knitter's craft.

Procedure. Essentially tailoring is a matter of fitting a chosen yarn and stitch to a particular shape. The basic procedure is to find out the number of stitches and rows in the relevant measurements – this is worked out by easy formulae based on your tension/gauge square – then cast on the right number of stitches, and increase or decrease them as you work, to create the required shape.

BODICES

The bodice of a garment can either be made straight or it can be shaped to fit body contours. Length can be whatever you choose, while width is determined by chest measurement plus the amount of ease (page 8).

STRAIGHT SHAPE

This is of course the simplest style of all, the length varying from a top cropped below bust line to a long mid-thigh sweater, or longer sweater-dress.

If the ease around the chest is considerable, then the lower edge of the sweater may need to be drawn in by the rib or other edging. These are explained in ribbings and edgings, page 89.

Side splits. An alternative to drawn-in edgings is side splits (photograph, page 33). Side splits can also be trimmed in another way (fig. 1), and in this case the lower edges of the bodice back and front are made 1½"–2" *narrower* than the required finished width, and the extra ¾"–1" cast on at each

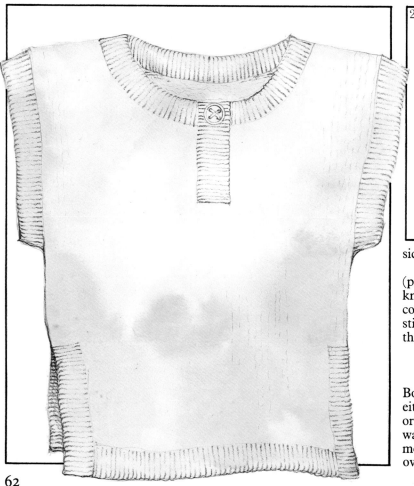

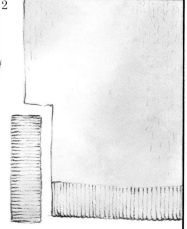

side at *top* of split (fig. 2).

Side-split edges are picked up (pick up and knit, page 16) and knitted *sideways*. The edging could be rib or garter or moss stitch, knitted on smaller needles than the main fabric.

WAISTED SHAPES

Bodices can be made to fit the waist either by tapering the bodice shape or by adding extra stitches at the waistband top, giving a fuller, more bloused shape (figs. 3 and 4 overleaf). Where the waistband

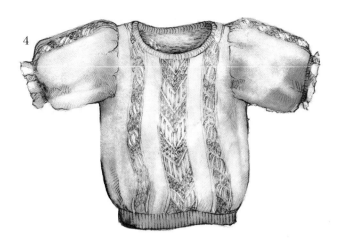

Tapered bodices are shaped between the waistband and chest (where armholes begin) and are made by increasing the number of stitches on bodice front and back at regular, evenly spaced intervals and on both edges of the work. Since this results in a 'stairstep' effect, it is often referred to as a stepped increase.

To calculate stepped increases you need to know how many stitches there will be at both waist and chest levels, given the tension/gauge you are working with; then how to space out the difference evenly between the two. Following instructions in the box opposite, this can be worked out easily, once you know your measurements and have made a tension/gauge square(s).

Note that with bodices it is usually better not to make the last increases too near the armhole.

tension/gauge is particularly tight, or the bodice tension/gauge particularly loose, a bloused effect may be achieved without any increase in stitches. (For more information see ribbings and edgings, page 89.)

When a different stitch is used for the waistband, e.g. rib, it is always necessary to knit a separate tension/gauge sample for that stitch.

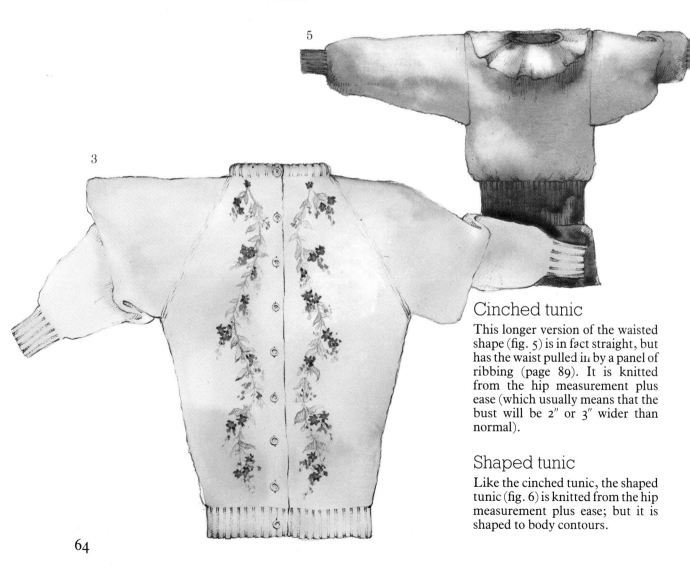

Cinched tunic

This longer version of the waisted shape (fig. 5) is in fact straight, but has the waist pulled in by a panel of ribbing (page 89). It is knitted from the hip measurement plus ease (which usually means that the bust will be 2″ or 3″ wider than normal).

Shaped tunic

Like the cinched tunic, the shaped tunic (fig. 6) is knitted from the hip measurement plus ease; but it is shaped to body contours.

6

7

To design knitwear, the following steps are necessary: each one is described in detail elsewhere in the book (and reference given here); so before you begin, make a thorough review of any area which you feel uncertain about.

1. You must decide upon the yarn type and needle size (endpapers), overall shape and features of the garment – including sleeve type, neckline, cuffs and hem (see this chapter).
2. Make a tension/gauge square(s), page 12).
3. Take body measurements and add 'ease' where necessary (pages 8–11), or measure an existing garment.
4. Draw a diagram and label garment measurements (page 10).
5. Convert required measurements: widths into stitches and lengths into rows, following conversion formulae below. Write results on diagrams.
6. Calculate total yarn requirement (page 16).
7. Knit up the pieces, and sew them together (Assembly, page 18).

Following calculation formulae below, the work is decreased evenly from hips to waist, then gradually increased to the desired chest measurement.

Peplums

Another variation of the waisted shape is the peplum (fig. 7), where the lower part of the bodice forms a frill round the hips. Frills normally measure 1½–2 times hip width and are decreased to required width at waist by one (or two) decreasing rows just below the waistline.

NECKLINES AND SLEEVES

Different styles of sleeve, neckline and collar, and how to design and make them, are described on the following pages. See also Colour and Texture, chapter 6, and Stitch Library, chapter 3, for yarn and stitch selection.

ESSENTIAL CALCULATIONS

To work out a knitting design or make alterations to patterns, garment measurements must be converted into numbers of stitches and rows, following the tension/gauge square – 4 inches square. (Note that while a tension/gauge *sample* may be any size, the tension/gauge *square* is always 4 inches square.)

Conversion of inches

This is accomplished by the following simple formulae.
To find out the number of stitches for a required width (for example to cast on at waist or cuff), multiply the desired measurement by the number of stitches in one row of your tension/gauge, then divide by 4 (width of t/g square).
To find out the number of rows in a required length: multiply the length measurement desired by the number of *rows* in your tension/gauge square, i.e. over 4″, and divide by 4 (length of t/g square).

Increases and decreases

Garments are shaped by increasing (decreasing) stitches at evenly spaced intervals between two different measurements and on both edges of work, e.g. tapered bodices.

First calculate the number of stitches in both measurements (widest and narrowest points), as described above.

The difference between the two is the number of stitches to be increased (decreased). Since these stitches must be added on (or subtracted from) both sides of the work, the number of rows on which increases are made will be only half that of the number of stitches involved. In other words, a difference between waist and chest of 12 stitches will mean increases at each end of 6 rows.
To find out which rows to increase (decrease), you need to know the number of rows (as well as difference in stitches) between the two measurements – between waist and chest for instance. (The method is described above.)

By dividing the number of rows to be affected by the number of increases or decreases (halved), you will discover *which* rows to make increases (decreases) on. For example: if there are 12 stitches to be increased (6 on each side of work) over 64 rows, you divide 64 by 6, and get 10 with 4 left over. This means you need to increase every 10 rows: for example, the 1st, 11th, 21st, 31st, 41st, 51st; leaving 13 more rows without shaping to complete the 64 rows required.

SLEEVES

Because they contribute so much to overall effect, sleeves are the most significant feature in knitwear design and different categories of sweater are named after them. Some sleeves are very easy to design and make – the T shape, the drop shoulder, even the batwing/dolmen. But those which require fitting a shaped sleeve head to the bodice – set-in sleeves and in particular the raglan – must be worked out with more intricate planning.

The photographs on pages 35–59 illustrate several versions of the five basic types of sleeve, and if you do not feel ready to launch forth with a design of your own from scratch, the accompanying step-by-step patterns can be used as templates: retaining the exact sleeve/armhole instructions and using the same tension/gauge, you can adapt other parts of the patterns to your own design. (See also, Adapting patterns, page 20.)

Sleeve design

In addition to choosing the *category* of sleeve, there is the tantalising question of shape: straight or tapered, long or short, loose or with cuffs, decorated or plain. (See also Colour and Texture and Stitch Library chapters.)

Straight, 'bloused' and most tapered sleeves are shaped between cuff and beginning of sleeve head by the same methods described for bodices between waist and chest, page 64. The sleeve head of your choice is added on and the armholes of the bodice shaped accordingly.

DROP SHOULDER

This is the simplest style of all, since neither the sleeve head nor the armhole (fig. 1) needs any shaping.

Drop shoulder garments should be made with plenty of chest ease (4″–6″) so that when the arm is down, the sweater is not bunched tightly underneath. Because the shoulder itself forms part of the sleeve, the actual sleeve length (F) is comparatively short; always B minus ½A. The minimum armhole depth (C or ½D) is roughly 7″–8″ for children and 9″–10″ for adults. (Mark back and front armhole base as a guide to assembly.)

The sleeve head (D) should as a rule measure twice the armhole depth (C), but by making it ½″ smaller (because it is more stretchy widthwise than the armhole edge is lengthwise), it will fit better.

Cast the sleeve head off loosely

1. The drop shoulder sleeve head is unshaped and the shoulder itself forms a part of the sleeve. The armhole base needs to be marked with a thread as a guide to assembly.

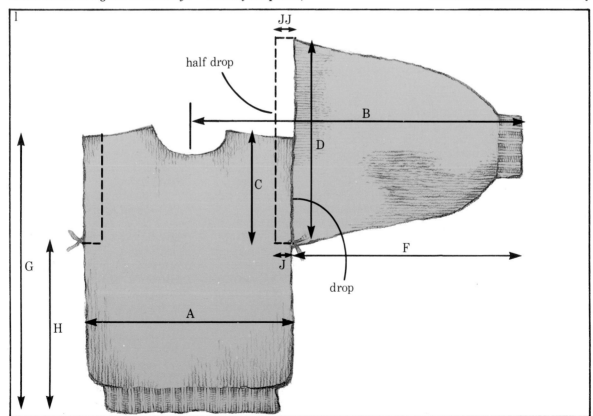

so that the seam will not be tight. (Use a size larger needle for a loose, elastic edge.)

The sleeve itself may be straight or tapered. If tapered, the required increases are made (as for tapered bodices, page 64) evenly up each side from cuff to top edge, roughly every 4th or 6th row. For details on working out increases, see Calculations, page 65.

Half drop shoulder

This shape is neater and rather less casual than the drop shoulder; and usually it fits more closely.

The sleeve head is set into the armhole in a rather simple fashion, and is itself unshaped (dotted line, fig. 1). The armhole is created by casting/binding off a few stitches (1″–2″) to make an indent (J).

When the sweater is designed to fit more closely than the drop shoulder, the chest width (A) often has 1″–2″ less ease. But it is also possible to have a very wide bodice, with as much as 6″–8″ ease, and, by adjusting J and JJ, to keep the shoulder seam on the point of the shoulder, or wherever desired. **Note** that the sleeve length (F) is increased by the same amount as the bodice is indented at armhole base (J); and the *side* edges of the extra sleeve length (JJ) are joined to the cast/bound off stitches of the armhole shaping.

In all other respects, proceed as for drop shoulder style.

T SHAPE

In the T shape, the sleeves form part of the knitted bodice.

The T shape is knitted in one piece or in two halves (illustrated by the dotted line in fig. 1). Knitting it in one piece avoids long, prominent seams across shoulders and down sleeves, and makes it easy to match regular stripes. It also enables you to knit from sleeve to sleeve as well as from front to back. Knitting in halves is more suitable for short sleeves or bulky/chunky yarns which make one-piece knitting unwieldy. Remember also that a patterned design or motif would come out upside down on one side of a bodice knitted in one piece.

T shapes need plenty of ease under arms: from 4″ to 6″ is normal. Note also that B = ½A + F, and G = H + C.

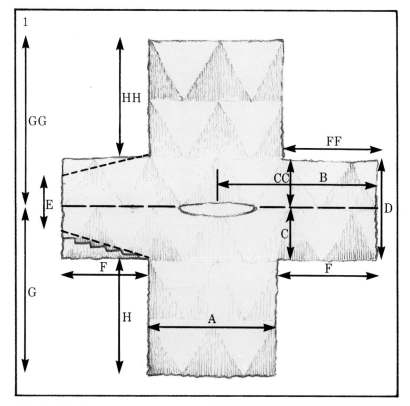

Straight sleeves

For a straight sleeve, cast on sleeve stitches (F) at length H, at the beginning of the next two rows.

Work to length G, making front neck shaping, if any, over last few rows. (A slash neck is often used for this shape, page 76.)

When neck is complete, work length CC (if knitting in one piece), then cast/bind off sleeve stitches (FF) at beginning of next two rows: knit HH to match H.

Tapered sleeves

Tapering is produced in two ways, depending on whether the garment is knitted from sleeve to sleeve or bodice to bodice.

Knitting from sleeve to sleeve, the increases are calculated and made following instructions on page 65, and the bodice cast on at length F, at the beginning of the next two rows. D minus E = the number of stitches to be increased (½ on each side of work) to form the first sleeve.

The 2nd sleeve must be worked in *corresponding decreases*.

When knitting the bodice (H) first, the stitches for sleeve length F are cast on in a series of gradual 'steps'. But since the stepped increases are built up *sideways* (fig. 2), the calculations are somewhat different.

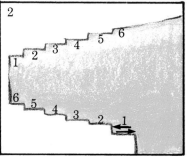

To find out the number of rows over which increases will be made, subtract ½E from C. Stitches should be divided as equally as possible between the number of steps required.

Since the groups of stitches can only be cast on at the *beginning* of rows, each 'step' will be 2 rows and the number of steps at each side will equal ½ the number of shaping rows.

Cast on stitches on right hand edge at beginning of right side rows and stitches on left hand edge at beginning of wrong side rows.

Corresponding groups of stitches are cast/bound off (beginning at length G + ½E) to shape the back.

Knitting two halves

Simply knit front to length G, and cast/bind off. Then knit back to length GG (from bottom to top), and join in the usual way.

BATWING/ DOLMAN

This is really an adaptation of the T shape with tapered sleeves previously described. But in order to make the sleeve much deeper, the sleeve stitches are increased along a curve which begins quite low, or near waist level.

The difference between batwing and dolman sleeves is one of degree; batwing being the more roomy. In fig. 1 the solid armhole curve represents the dolman shape and the broken lines, batwing. Like the T shape, this shape can be knitted in one piece, or in two halves.

The disadvantage of the style is that it cannot be worn underneath most coats and jackets.

SLEEVE SHAPING

The sleeve curve should be plotted with the aid of graph paper, as in fig. 2 (see page 95 for instructions how to use).

To find out the total number of stitches to cast on for each sleeve (length E), subtract half of C from B. If therefore B is 26″ and C is 20″, then E = 26 minus ½ of 20. 16″. If the t/g square is 16 sts to 4″ (¼ of the total measurement), then 4 × 16 sts = 64 stitches to be cast on.

To chart the curve, find out the number of rows in F by subtracting H from G, and convert to rows (see Calculations page 65).

Using each square of graph paper as one stitch/row, number the squares vertically for F and horizontally for E. Then draw a curve which describes the sleeve curve you have in mind. Stitches can be marked in over it with a coloured pencil, as shown.

Increases

The stitches are added on in four

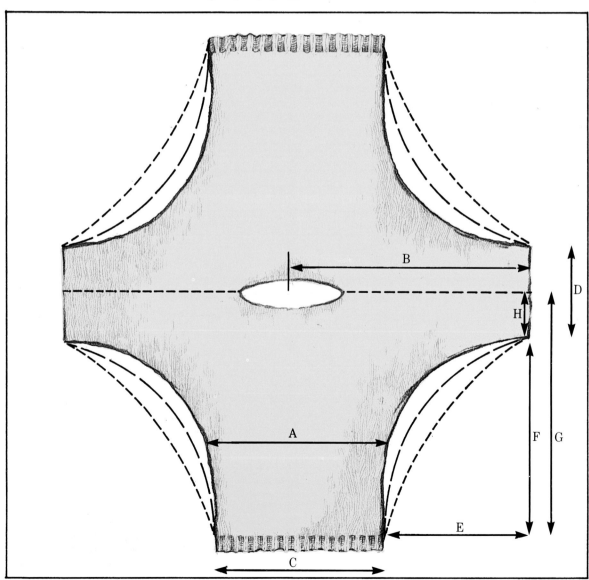

different groupings to make sleeves. These groupings do not have a precise formula, but the progression given below represents a close guideline to follow. The point is to cover the distance required, making as smooth a stitch curve as you can. Note that the steeper the curve desired, the longer the 'step'.

First increases. Make these in fairly steep 'steps' 1″ or 2″ apart (increasing 1 stitch at both edges every 4th or 6th row).

Second increases. For another quarter or so of the curve make increases closer together, on every alternate row.

Third increases. Near the centre of curve begin to make them on every row.

Fourth increases. Towards the end of the curve, cast on stitches in small *groups* to reach the required sleeve length. The wider the 'step' the straighter the line will be.

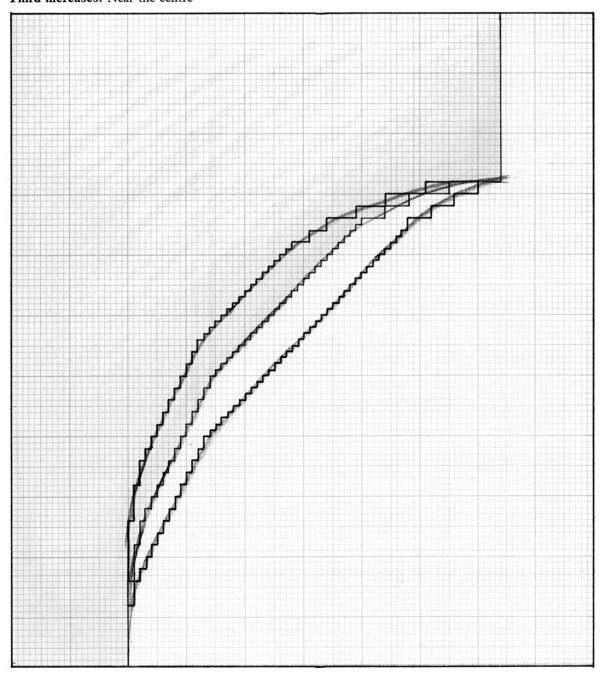

SET-IN SLEEVE

The set-in sleeve takes the half drop shoulder one step further by adding a *sloping angle* to its armhole indentation (fig. 1) and putting a curve on the sleeve head to make a better fit. This is the classic sweater shape, suitable for wearing under a jacket or coat, and ease round the chest need be only about 2″. But if a looser fit is desired, the measurements A B D and H should all be increased and the sleeve head M reduced by the amount B is enlarged.

Note also that ½B (shoulder width) + M (sleeve head depth) + L (underarm sleeve length) = C (centre back neck to cuff when measure with arm flat to side of body (fig. 2). Therefore, the wider you make B, the shorter M must be.

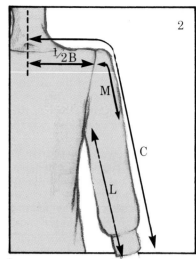

ARMHOLES

The shaping at each side of bodice is formed at length F. The total measurement to be decreased is A minus B, and half this amount (G) must be decreased at each side.

Indent. Cast/bind off a small group of stitches (O) – approximately ½″–1″ – at each side. (Ad-just measurement if necessary to correspond with a stitch pattern.)

Make the sloping angle (N) by decreasing sharply, e.g. at each end of every alternate row, until stitches for B remain.

Work to length E, shaping neck (page 78) and shoulders (opposite).

SLEEVE HEAD

The aim is to make the curved edge of the sleeve head the same length as the curve of the armhole (red

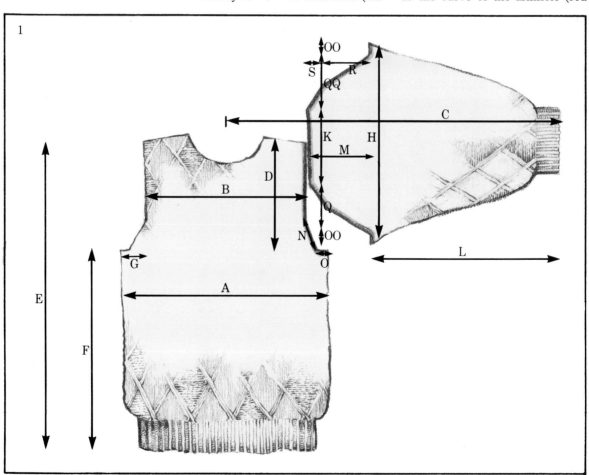

line in fig. 1). There is no precise way to work this out, which in some ways makes it easier to do. A little extra length on a sleeve head can, depending somewhat on the style, be eased into the armhole. And if you shape one sleeve head at a time, you can make sure it is right before working the other.

Measurements

Make flat top of sleeve (K) 3″ to 5″ wide. This is an arbitrary measurement; it cannot be calculated.

Sleeve head depth M = C minus L, minus ½B.

Convert measurement H and K into stitches, and measurement M into rows (Calculations, page 65), then draw a diagram of the shape and write down conversion results.

Shaping sleeve head

First work to length L. Then cast/bind off indent OO at each side equal to O.

By subtracting the number of stitches in K from the number of stitches on needle, you will know how many stitches to decrease between OO and K. Half these stitches (Q) will be decreased at each side, over the number of rows in M.

Decreases are usually made in two parts. The lower decreases (R), at each end of every *alternate* row, and the upper decreases (S) at each end of every row.

To find out the number of rows with decreases at each end of every row (S), the formula is twice Q, minus M = S. In other words, subtract the rows in sleeve head M from the number of stitches to be decreased in all.

To find out the number of rows with decreases every alternate row (R), the formula is M minus S = R. Subtract the number with decreases each end of every row (S) from number of rows in sleeve head (M).

You now know the number of rows in both R and S.

Cast/bind off remaining stitches (K). This completes the sleeve head.

Puff sleeve

In this set-in sleeve, the curve of the sleeve head is considerably larger than the armhole curve.

The excess is gathered or pleated around the top half of armhole (fig. 3) when sewing in the sleeve.

Measurements H and K should be 2″–4″ larger than for classic set-in style, and sleeve depth M about 2″ longer.

SHAPING SHOULDERS

It is usual for garments with set-in sleeves to have shaped, sloping shoulders for a neater fit; but other styles such as dolman/batwing can also be shaped in this way.

MEASUREMENT

The shoulder slope depth (D in fig. 3) rarely alters more than ½″. A useful guide is ¾″ for children, 1″ for women, and 1¼″ for men.

Note also that while width A = twice C, plus B; width C = A minus B, divided by 2.

Convert A, B and C to stitches, and D to rows, in order to calculate shaping (page 65).

DECREASES

The shaping is accomplished by a series of 'stepped' decreases made evenly across each shoulder. In order to make these 'steps' less obvious, slip 1st stitch of 2nd and following 'steps' at each side. Cast/bind off in the usual way.

Without breaking the yarn on every row, stitches can only be cast/bound off at the *beginning* of a row. Therefore, bodice back right shoulder (as worn) will be cast/bound off at beginning of right side rows, and left shoulder (as worn) at beginning of wrong side rows. Front shoulders – opposite of back.

To find out the number of 'steps' (rows with decreases) on each shoulder, divide the number of rows in D by 2, in other words, ½D.

Then divide the number of stitches to be cast/bound off on each shoulder (C) by the number of 'steps' (½ the rows). For example: 25 stitches over 8 rows (4 steps) would mean 3 decreases of 6 stitches and 1 decrease of 7 stitches.

WORKING

Shoulder shapings on the front should match those on the back. The left shoulder (as worn) is usually worked first, and stitches (as for back) decreased at beginning of right side rows.

For the right shoulder (as worn), the groups of stitches are decreased at beginning of wrong side rows.

Casting/binding off

On wrong side rows of st st, this should be worked purlwise; or in K and P as set for a stitch pattern.

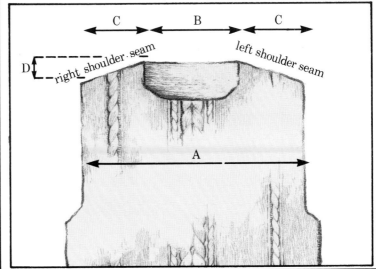

SADDLE SHOULDER

In the saddle shoulder style (fig. 1) an extension of the sleeve head (N) forms a 'saddle' between bodice front and back, shortening their lengths proportionately. The width of the saddle can vary, but the finished length of the sweater (E) is always F + D + ½P.

Saddle, shoulders can be applied to drop or half drop shoulders, as in figs. 2 and 3, as well as to set-in sleeves (fig. 1). Saddles make a good base for decorative or contrasting panels up the centre of sleeves, as the cable panel shows. A wide saddle may also be shaped to form part of the neckline (fig. 2). **Work front and back** to length F and shape armholes according to sleeve type, also front neck if desired. Cast/bind off stitches at length E minus ½P.

Narrow saddle

Work sleeve and sleeve head as previously described until only the stitches for flat top of sleeve (K in fig. 1) remain.

Leaving stitches required for saddle at centre of sleeve top, cast/bind off the stitches on each side. Then work saddle stitches to length N, and cast/bind off.

Wide saddle

In this version (fig. 2) the saddle is 2 or 3 times wider than for fig. 1, and the saddle ends are used to shape the neckline. Note that half of P forms part of the neck shaping (Necklines, page 76), and the other half, part of the centre back.

The two saddles are joined at the back by a small seam, or by button loops.

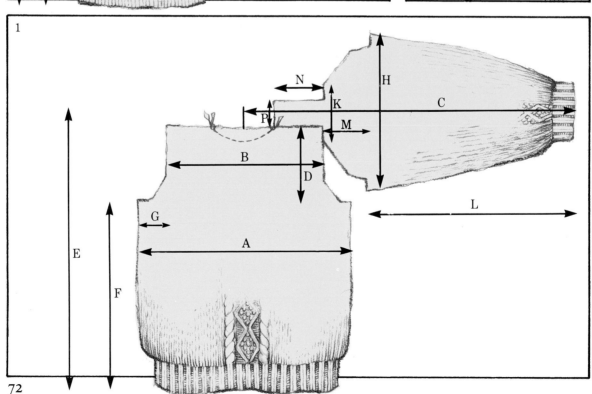

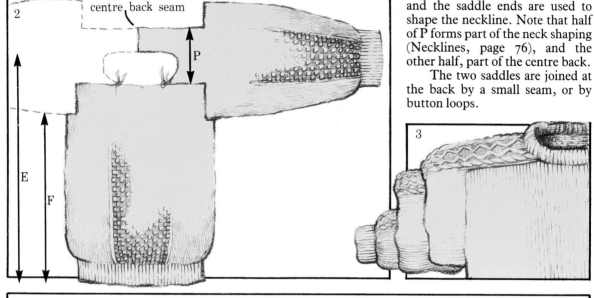

RAGLAN

In the raglan shape the entire sleeve head is extended to the neckline, and forms a part of the shoulder (fig. 1). The depth of both armhole (C) and sleeve head (M) are exactly the same and will contain therefore the same number of rows.

Measurements

Once the armhole depth (C) is decided upon, other measurements can develop from this. Length C is usually 6″–7″ for children and 8″–9″ for adults.

As a rule the top of sleeve width G measures between 1″–3″.

Be sure to take the following points into consideration also, when working out pattern measurements:

The finished length of bodice front/back N = K minus ½G, while K is the finished length of *garment*.

L = K minus ½G and C.

B = ½D + M + H.

The finished armhole depth = C + ½G.

J and JJ are normally ½″–1″.

Calculate bodice and sleeve lengths by the methods previously described in this chapter.

SHAPING

Raglans – which refers both to sleeve head and armhole shapings – are formed by decreases over a steep curve, and these need to be worked out on graph paper as shown overleaf. (For instructions on using graph paper, see page 95). **Raglan decreases** are normally made using paired decreases (page 15) sloping to the left on right hand edges, and to the right on left hand edges. Therefore, for st st on right side rows, begin skpo, end K2tog. On wrong side rows, begin P2tog, end P2tog tbl.

In order to give the decreased edge of the raglan a neat border along the seams, it is advisable to make all the decreases in a line 1 or 2 (or 3) stitches in from the outside edge.

To plot the armhole shaping, number the rows in C vertically on graph paper as shown, making the drawing as wide as the number of

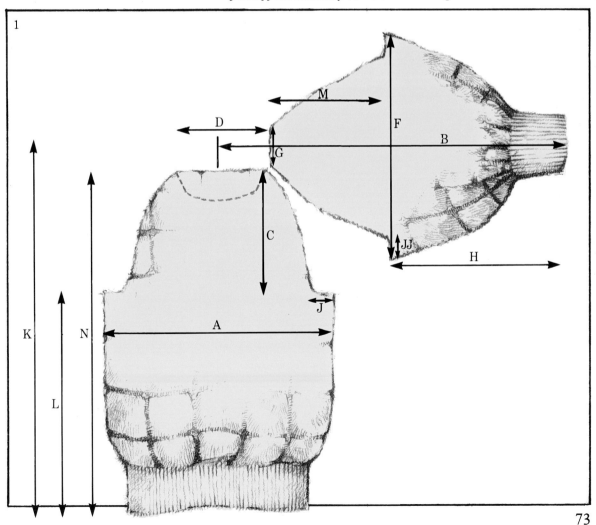

stitches in A (1 square = 1 stitch). Draw in J (usually ½″–1″).

Armholes

The front and back are worked alike except that the front neckline must be shaped (page 76).

As indicated on the graph, the lower stitches (R) in the armhole curve are decreased every other row and upper stitches (S) on every row.

To find out the number of rows with decreases in R and S, the formulae are as follows: S = twice Q minus C, and R = C minus S.

Sleeves

Sleeves are shaped similarly to armholes, but although both have the same number of rows, there usually are more stitches to decrease in sleeves.

When length H is reached, cast/bind off JJ at each side to match J.

To find out the number of decreases, subtract stitches in G from remaining stitches. Half that number will be decreased at each side.

Remember that decreases are worked more closely together towards the top of the raglan shaping.

To find out the number of rows with decreases in SS and RR (fig. 2), the formulae are the same as for raglan back/front (and set-in sleeve head).

NECKBAND

Note that final round neck measurement = width at top of back D + twice top of sleeve width G + measurement round front neckline.

It is usual for stitches at neckline to be put on a holder, and when raglan seams have been sewn together the neckband stitches are picked up and knitted (page 16) to make the neckband or collar (page 77).

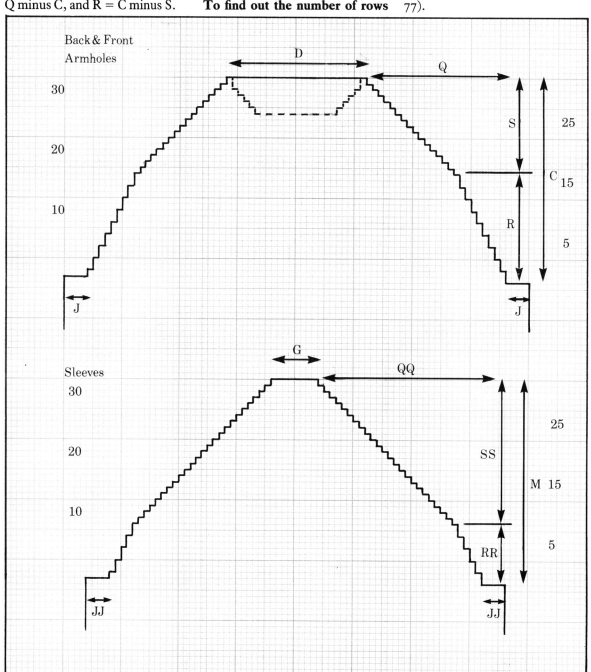

74

HEMS

Knitted hems can be worked on cuffs, straight neck edgings and pocket tops in addition to the bottom edge of garments. But unlike ribbing, hems are not elastic, and therefore should never be used where a tight fitting edge is needed.

In order to make the hem lie flat, hem rows should be worked on needles 1–2 sizes smaller than main needles. And it is best to work a special row to make the fold line.

Hem allowance is normally 1″ to 1½″.

St st hem

Fig. 1 shows a st st hem. Using smaller needles, work hem length, ending wrong side (P) row.
Fold line row: P on right side row.

Change to main needles and work main part as required.

Stitch pattern hem

When using a stitch pattern, a slip stitch fold line is more suitable for the hem.

On smaller needles, work hem rows in st st, ending wrong side (P) row.
Fold line row: *K1, bring yarn to front of work, sl 1, take yarn to back of work, K1 * repeat from * to * to end.

Change to main needles and work main part.

Picot hem

A picot hem (fig. 2) is most often used for baby garments and other delicate work.

On smaller needles, work hem rows in st st as described above, ending wrong side (P) row.
Fold line row: *K2tog, yrn/yo* repeat from * to * ending K1 or K2.

Change to main needles and work main part as required.

STITCHING

When garment is complete, fold up hem allowance along fold line row and stitch hem in position, matching each stitch of cast on edge to the back of 1 stitch of main part, working along a straight row of stitches, as in fig. 1.

Neckband, pocket hems. On garments where the hem is formed at the *end* of work, do not cast/bind off, but sew down by the stitch-for-stitch method shown in fig. 2.

Slip stitch each stitch from needle to corresponding stitch of main part. This is less bulky than casting/binding off the edge and then sewing it down.

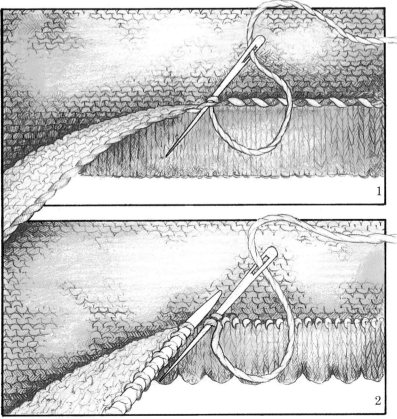

NECKLINES AND COLLARS

Before you begin to knit the front and back of a garment, you must decide upon the style of neckline, and find out which row to begin the shaping on. (The back neck is not often shaped.)

Remember that the neck must be big enough for a head to get through, otherwise the design must include a fastening device. Children's heads are much larger in proportion to their bodies than are adults, and for this reason children's knitwear tends more often to have neck or shoulder fastenings attached.

Shaped necklines are based on rectangles, the front edges being either rounded or sliced off to make a curve or a V shape, or else left as a square (see diagram). The shaping is accomplished by decreasing stitches, and the decreases should generally slope outwards towards the shoulders (see page 15).

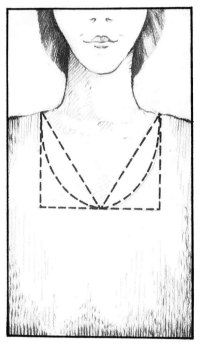

Necklines derive from rectangles. Edges are rounded or sliced to a V.

In order to plan a neckline, the neck opening measurements must first be converted into stitches and rows, using *main* tension/gauge. The method for converting inches into stitches and rows, and for calculating the number of decreases (increases) and where to put them, is given on page 65.

Edgings are very often used to trim necklines and they can produce a variety of decorative touches. They also have a practical use. By adding an edging in a different tension/gauge, e.g. a rib, the neckline will be pulled in slightly, making it fit more closely while retaining the necessary head fit (Ribbing and edgings, page 89).

SLASH NECK

The simplest neck of all, the slash neck (fig. 1), is often applied to drop shoulder shapes (photograph, page 35). The back and front necklines are cast/bound off straight across (with or without shoulder shaping, page 71), the shoulder seams (C) are joined and the neck edge allowed to roll.

Since there is no shaping, neck width A must be wide enough to fit over the head, or the shoulder seams must be fastened with buttons.

Several variations of the slash neck described below give a pleasing decorative effect and, in some instances, a neater, closer fit.

Rib edge

In this version (fig. 2), ribbing ensures that the neck edge will lie flat.

The last 1″ or 2″ *and* the shoulder shaping (page 71) of back and front are worked in rib, using needles two sizes smaller than for main part (Ribbing and edgings, page 89).

Overlapping shoulders

In fig. 3, the bodice back and front are shown opened out flat to illustrate how rib edges may be overlapped at the shoulders.

Make the ribbing 1″ deep and include *half* this rib edge depth (D) as part of required armhole depth (E). Note that, overlapping, front and back ribbed borders will measure D.

Work rib with smaller needles (Ribbing and edgings, page 89).

There is no shoulder shaping.

Button shoulders

Instead of sewing shoulders together, one or both may be closed with buttons and buttonholes (page 87) or button loops along cast/bound off edge of front.

The example shown (fig. 4) is in garter stitch, which is often used to trim slash neck edges.

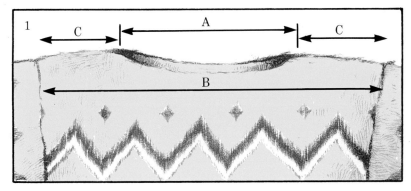

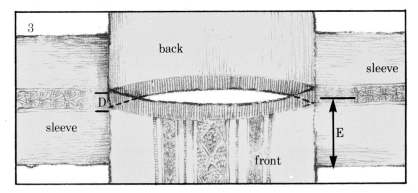

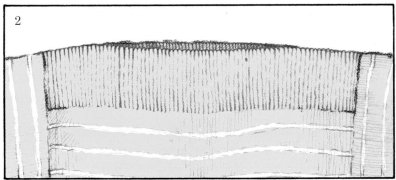

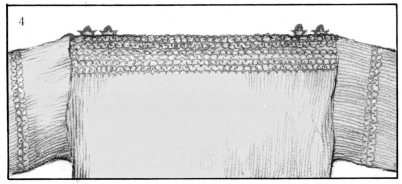

PICKING UP NECKLINE STITCHES

To make a neck edging, stitches from the shaped parts of the neckline (which have been cast/bound off) must be picked up and knitted, together with those stitches which have been left on a holder.

To find out how many stitches to pick up and knit, measure the curve or V with a tape measure, then convert the measurement into stitches, using *main* tension/gauge and following conversion formulae on page 65. Pick up and knit these stitches (page 16).

Stitch pattern adjustments. If the edging pattern involves a specific number of stitches, e.g. K2 P2, a multiple of 4 stitches to be repeated throughout, then the *total* number of stitches in the neck edge must be calculated in advance and, if necessary, an adjustment made by increasing or decreasing the number of stitches to be picked up and knitted.

V NECKS

V-neck shaping often begins at the same level as armhole shaping (fig. 1). The back neck is not usually shaped.

Note that the number of stitches which must be decreased in order to make the neck opening equals the number of stitches in the back neck (A). If there are 42 stitches in the back neck, then 42 stitches must be decreased across the bodice front, *half of them on each side of the neckline.*

On average, back neck width (A), below ribbing, measures 4″–5″ for children, 5½″–6½″ for women, and 6″–7″ for men. While front neck depth (B) measures, for children, 6″–8″; adults, 8″–9½″.

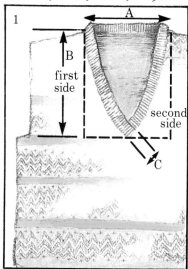

To find out the number of stitches and rows to be decreased, width A must first be converted into stitches, and length B into rows, using tension/gauge square and following instructions on page 65. These instructions also explain how to place decreases evenly along the rows. Note that it is preferable in V necks not to make decreases too near the tops of shoulders.

WORKING

Knit bodice back, shaping armholes (and shoulders if desired, page 71), then slip back neck stitches on to a holder or spare needle.

Knit bodice front up to row beginning front neck opening, ending wrong side row.
1st side: next row: work to centre and turn. Then work on these stitches only, decreasing as calculated, and shaping armholes and shoulders as desired.

2nd side: with right side facing, rejoin yarn at right of remaining stitches and complete to match 1st side, reversing all shapings.

EDGING

V neck edgings are worked either on a circular needle or a set of 4 double-ended needles (instructions, page 16). A circular needle should measure 2″ shorter than the measurement round neckline edge.

Ribbed neck edging is usually worked on needles 2 sizes smaller than the main part, and cast/bound off in the rib pattern. See also Ribbing and edging, page 89.

The ribbed edging in fig. 1 is worked in *rows*, turning each row at centre front.

Overlap and sew down side edges at centre front.

Stitches for edging
Neckline edging is worked on back neck stitches which have been put on a holder, and on stitches which must be picked up along the V shape.

To find out how many stitches to pick up on each side of the V, see instructions in the box on page 77.
Working edging Join shoulder seams and pick up and knit stitches between centre front and shoulder seam; then knit stitches from back neck holder; finally pick up and knit the stitches from other shoulder down to centre front.

Deep rib

The neckline shown in fig. 2 is exactly like that in fig. 1, except that the rib is made to a depth of 3″–4″, then doubled over and stitched to the inside.

Classic V neck

This style (fig. 3) is also similar to fig. 1, but instead of overlapping, the centre front ribbing is decreased to form a flat edge (photograph, page 53).

When knitting the bodice front, leave 1 stitch at centre front on a safety pin before shaping the front neck edges. Ideally, the bodice front should have an odd number of stitches, so that both sides of the front neck shaping will be equal.

Edging
The neck edging is worked in *rounds*, not rows, decreasing 1

stitch at each side of centre front on every round, and using any of the paired methods described on page 15.

For K1 P1 rib edge, work as follows: pick up and knit stitch from pin, then remaining neckline stitches as described above (even number of stitches in all).

Round 1: K centre front st from pin; P2tog tbl, ⋆ K1, P1⋆ repeat ⋆ to ⋆ to 3 sts before centre front st; K1, P2tog.

Round 2: K centre front st; P2tog tbl, ⋆P1,K1⋆ repeat ⋆ to ⋆ to 3 sts before centre front st; P1 P2tog.

Repeat these 2 rounds for depth required; cast/bind off in rib, decreasing 1 st at each side of centre front stitch.

V neck collars

In fig. 4, the neck is shaped as in fig. 1 and the edging made as in fig. 2, but not sewn down.

Fig. 5 shows the same collar joined at centre front with a seam for about half its depth.

Collars may also be made with a contoured edge, giving greater depth at back of neck. Instructions, page 83.

Short wide V

Fig. 6 illustrates a short, wide V neck style which is useful for matching sloping lines of a stitch pattern.

Its depth and width may be varied as desired, so long as the opening is large enough for the head.

The overall method is the same as for fig. 1, but keep in mind that the shorter the V is made, the wider the neck must be.

Filled V

Fig. 7 shows a V neck filled in with a triangle of rib. The triangular piece is best worked separately, matching the increasing side edges to the slope of the decreasing front edges, and sewn in afterwards.

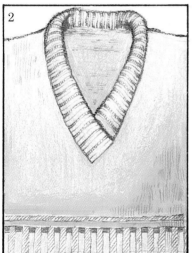

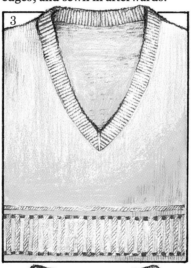

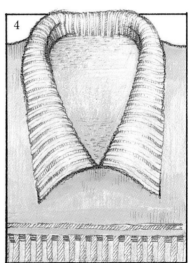

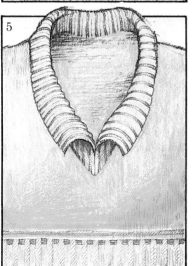

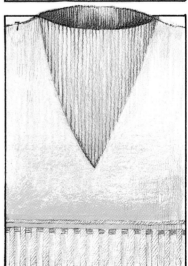

ROUND NECKS

The main point to keep in mind with round necks is that they must be large enough to fit easily over the head.

MEASURING

In classic round neck sweaters (fig. 1), the back neck width (A) and front neck width (B) are equal. The neck depth (F) is up to half this measurement.

As a rule of thumb, the average back neck width below edging for a child is 5″–6″; for a woman, 6″–7″; and for a man, 7″–8″. The front shapings (D and E) are about 1″.

If you are worried that a neckline will end up being too large or small, take neck measurements from another sweater, preferably one with a similar tension/gauge, so that stretch will be roughly the same.

WORKING

Following fig. 1 and the formulae on page 65, first convert A, C and D into stitches and E and F into rows. Then calculate decreases required to shape curve. (Note that D = stitches to be decreased to make curve, and E the number of rows over which decreases are made.)

Front neck

First work bodice front to length of bodice back minus front neck depth F, shaping armholes as required, and ending wrong side row.

1st side: Work stitches to right of C (as they face you). Turn. Work on these stitches only, decreasing 1 stitch at neck edge on every row, or as required, until stitches in D

have been decreased.

Complete to same length as back, shaping the shoulders if necessary.

2nd side: With right side of work facing, slip centre front stitches (C) on to a holder and rejoin yarn at right of remaining stitches.

Complete the row. Work remaining stitches to match left side (reversing all shapings).

EDGING

The neck edge shown in fig. 1 may be worked on 2 needles, a circular or 4 double-ended needles.

To calculate the number of stitches needed to make the edging, see box on page 79.

Two-needle method. Join shoulder seam of back and 1st side.

With right side of work facing, and using needles 2 sizes smaller than main part, knit up the back neck stitches (A) from holder. Then pick up and knit stitches from G on 1st side; knit up centre front stitches (C) and pick up and knit stitches from G on other side.

Work rib rows until required depth is reached, and cast/bind off in rib, or work double crew neck described below.

Join other shoulder seam and neck edge seam.

Circular knitting. Join both shoulder seams, then pick up and knit stitches for neck edge as described above, but work in rounds instead of rows.

Doubled crew neck

Work twice the depth described above, then fold the neckband in half to inside and sew it down neatly. Make sure sewing is loose

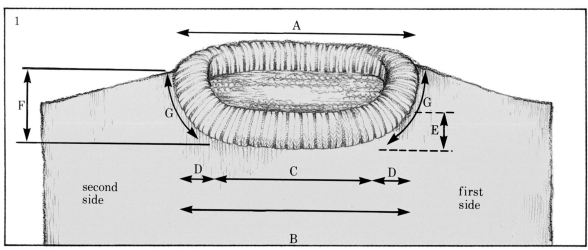

enough for neck edge to fit easily over head.

Polo neck

With polo necks (fig. 2), the front neck depth (F) is usually quite shallow – 1½″–2″ less than for a conventional round neck, and the back neck width and front neck edge (A and C in fig. 1) must be increased proportionately to make the neck circumference big enough.

Polo necks can be worked to any depth required and folded over one or more times.

Funnel neck

This round neck edge, (fig. 3) is worked in st st instead of rib, and when cast/bound off the edge forms a roll with P side out.

To work this edge in circular rounds, knit every round.

Cowl neck

In this version (fig. 4), the front neck (F in fig. 1) is shallow, as for the polo neck, but the neck widths (A and B in fig. 1) are increased to as much as 10″, to make a large, floppy neck.

Round collar

The example in fig. 5 is worked using either a circular needle or 4 double-ended needles (page 16).

Pick up neck stitches beginning and ending at centre front, then turn every row at centre front until required depth. See page 83 for methods of shaping a collar.

Boat neck

A wide, shallow neck (fig. 6) shaped in a curve at back edge as well as in the front.

Follow the instructions for basic round neck given above, but make A about 10″, and D about ⅓ of A. F = depth of shoulder shaping.

Scoop neck

A summer or evening neckline, (fig. 7) has a deep scoop in front and the back shaped as for boat neck above. Note that D = ⅓A, and depth of shaping E about ⅓ of total neck depth F.

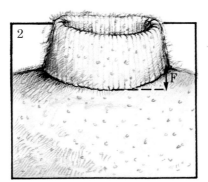

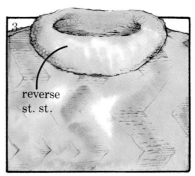

reverse st. st.

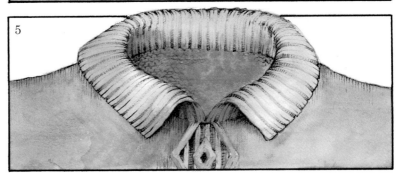

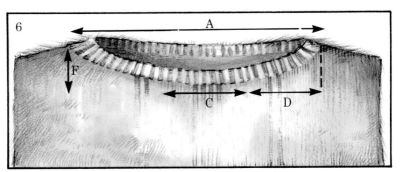

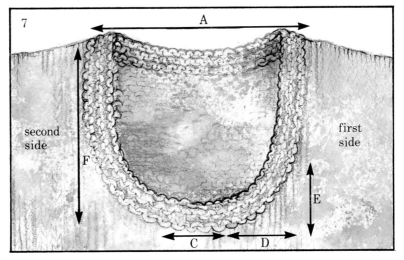

SHAWL COLLARS

The shawl collar usually fills a rectangular neck opening in which back and front necklines are the same width and contain the same number of stitches. The neck depth (B in fig. 1) often begins at armhole level.

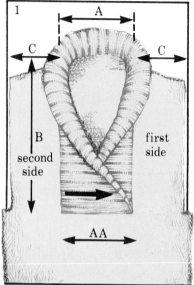

NECKLINE

The back neckline is roughly the same width as for V neck garments already described. The back neck stitches are left on a holder after working shoulder shaping (page 71). (Back necklines are not normally shaped.)

Front neckline
Work bodice to length required minus front neck opening B, and ending wrong side row.
1st side. Next row: work number of stitches required for shoulder (C). Turn. Work these stitches to length required, shaping shoulder to match back.
2nd side. With right side facing, rejoin yarn at right of remaining stitches and *cast/bind off centre front stitches* (A).

Work 2nd side to match 1st, reversing shapings.

NECK INSET

The neck inset can be made in a number of styles and worked either vertically or horizontally. A circular needle or a set of 4 double-ended needles 2 sizes smaller than main part should be used for horizontally worked insets (figs. 2, 3, 5).

82

Horizontal rib collar

Using rib tension/gauge, and following conversion instructions for stitches (page 77), calculate the number of stitches to be picked up from side neck edge (B, fig. 1).

Join shoulder seams and, with right side of work facing, pick up and knit stitches from 2nd side of front neck depth (B); then knit stitches from back neck (A) and pick up and knit stitches from the other front neck edge (side 1). Note that no stitches are knitted up from centre front (AA).

Turn. Work in rib rows to a depth equal to front neck width AA. (Shape collar if required. See opposite.)

Cast/bind off in rib.

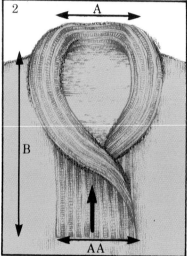

Vertical rib collar

In this version (fig. 2), it is the back neck stitches that are cast/bound off and the front neck stitches which are left on a holder – the reverse of the previous version.
Note: it is advisable to join garment shoulder seams and, while knitting collar, to sew one long edge of it to neckline edge as you work (page 11). This will ensure an accurate fit.

Working
With right side of front facing and using needles 2 sizes smaller than main part, knit across front neck stitches on holder, increasing as many stitches evenly across the row as is necessary to keep front neck width constant in spite of tighter tension/gauge.

For example: if front neck width (AA) is 6″ and 42 stitches at main tension/gauge and the rib tension/gauge is 32 stitches over 4″, then in rib, AA = (6″ × 32) ÷ 4,

or 48 stitches at rib/tension gauge. A difference of 6 stitches to be added on across the first row of neck edge.

Work in required rib stitch on these stitches until piece measures twice front neck depth (B), plus back neck width (A).

Cast/bind off in rib and sew cast/bound off edge to front neck stitches, behind the first collar row.

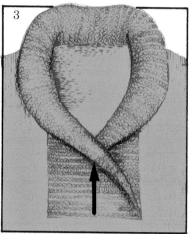

A vertical collar may also be knitted in garter stitch as in fig. 3.

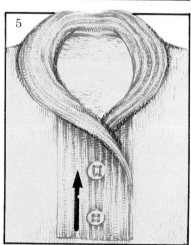

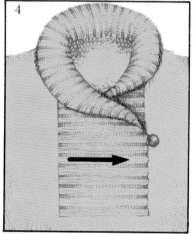

Button shawl collars

Figs. 4 and 5 are worked like figs. 1 and 2 respectively, except that buttons hold the collar overlaps in place (see Buttonholes, page 87).

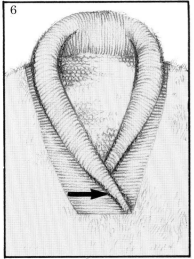

Blunted V neck

The front neck of this style (fig. 6) is similar to a V neck, page 79), but several stitches are cast/bound off at centre front to make a flat-bottomed V.

The stitches are picked up as for V-neck edge, and worked in rows to depth required, usually shaping collar edge (see opposite) to give greater depth at centre back neck. (It is not necessary to shape side edges of collar.)

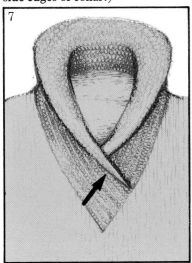

V shawl collar

The front neck edges of this garment (fig. 7) are the same as for a V neck, page 79. Make the collar as described for fig. 6, using garter stitch if preferred, and sew side edges of the collar rows to front neck edges over required length, overlapping as shown.

To make a collar, stitches round the neckline are either picked up, as described on page 77, and knitted, or the collar is knitted separately and sewn on as a separate piece.

Collars may of course be knitted up as a straight band, but they may also be given contours which make the back neck deeper and the short front edges fit together more closely.

Fig. 1 shows a collar laid out flat. The stitches at the front edge (B) can be increased – usually 1″ to 2″ each side – by evenly spaced increases (page 14). It is important to make these increases neatly; working them either 1, 2 or 3 stitches in from each edge (according to stitch pattern) and using the method for invisible increases described on page 14.

Shaping top edge

When the short edges of the collar have been increased, the back edge (H) may then be shaped, making it deeper by amount D.

Make F at each side approximately ¼H (total width).

Convert D and F to rows and stitches respectively, and calculate shaping rows as for shaped shoulders (page 71). However, the groups of stitches are not cast/bound off at the beginning of rows, but left *unworked* at *end* of rows (fig. 2), turning the work and slipping 1st stitch before working back.

When shaping is complete, work to end of one row, then work another row across all the stitches before casting/binding off.

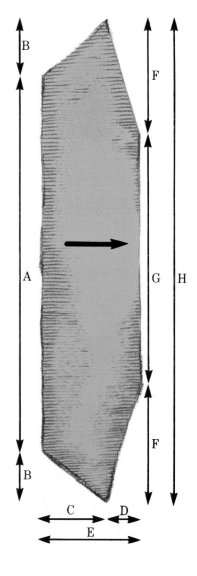

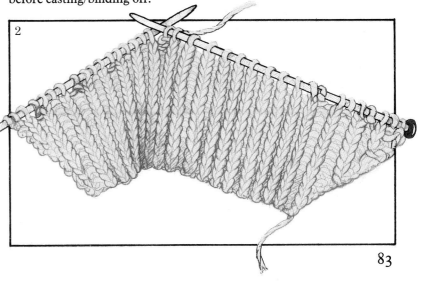

BUTTON FRONTS

A variation usually of round necklines, button fronts enable neckbands and collars to fit more closely. And since they can be worn open as well as fastened, they contribute a certain flexibility of style.

MEASUREMENTS

Following fig. 1 and the instructions for round necklines (page 80), decide the measurements for C, D and H, and convert to stitches. Note that C + 2D + 2H = A (back neck width).

Convert E, F and J into rows.

NECKLINE

The back neck is not usually shaped. Work as described for round neck and leave the stitches on a holder.

Front neck

Work to beginning of button band opening, ending wrong side row.

1st side. Next row: work stitches for shoulder + D and H. Turn. Work on these stitches to complete length J, ending wrong side row.

Work stitches for shoulder + D. Turn. Leave stitches for H on a holder.

Decrease 1 stitch at neck edge on every row (or as required) until stitches D have all been decreased and stitches for shoulder remain.

Work to match length of back, ending wrong side row and shaping shoulder (page 71).

2nd side. With right side of front facing, rejoin yarn at right of remaining stitches and *cast/bind off centre front stitches* (C).

Complete to match other side, reversing all shapings.

EDGING

The ribbed neck edging shown in fig. 1 is worked using 2 needles 2 sizes smaller than for main part. To calculate the number of stitches needed to make the edging, see box on page 77.

Join shoulder seams.

With right side of work facing, and beginning at 2nd side of front neck opening: knit up stitches from holder (H); pick up and knit stitches from neck edge G; knit up stitches from back neck (A) and continue round neck edge of 1st side to match 2nd side.

Work neck edging rows to depth required – in this instance equal to C.

Cast/bind off in rib pattern.

Button band

This is positioned on left side of the garment (as worn) for a woman, and the reverse for a man.

Width of band in fig. 1 = J + depth of neck edge.

Convert measurement to stitches (page 77). Then, with right side of front facing and using needles 2 sizes smaller than for main part, pick up and knit stitches evenly from side edge of front opening, including neck edging rows.

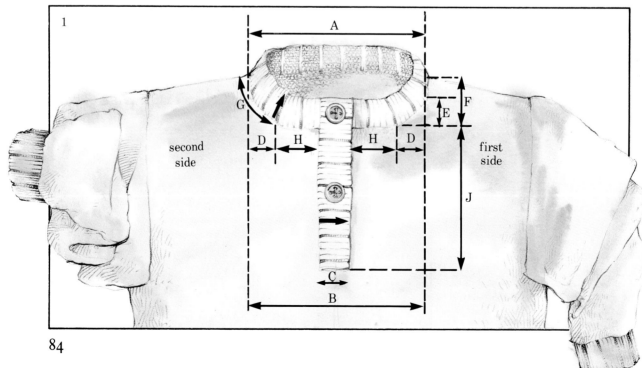

Work to depth C. Cast/bind off in rib pattern.

Buttonhole band
Pick up and knit from opposite side, the same number of stitches as for button band.

Work band to half depth required (½C), then work buttonholes in next row (instructions, page 87), and work to depth required (C).

Cast/bind off as above.

Sew the side edges of the two bands to the cast/bound off centre front stitches (C), with buttonhole band on top.

Button front collar

In this example (fig. 2), the bodice back and front are worked in the same way as for the basic button front above, but the centre front stitches of the bodice (width C), are left on a holder, then worked vertically from C.

Button band. Cast on stitches (C) with smaller needles and work to required length (J in fig. 1). Leave stitches on a holder.

Buttonhole band. Stitches are knitted up from centre front stitches (C) and the buttonhole band worked as for button band. To match buttonholes to button positions, see page 87. Again, leave stitches on holder at length required.

Collar. The neck edge is then worked by knitting up buttonhole band stitches, all neck edge stitches as for basic button front, and button band stitches.

Knit collar to desired depth. (For a shaped collar, see page 83.)

Asymmetrical

Worked as for fig. 1, the buttonhole band in fig. 3 is placed on one side, next to front neck shaping (D).

Zip opening

Unlike the above example, no stitches are cast/bound off at front of bodice to make the neck opening: the stitches are simply divided at this point and worked as 2 sides.

Note that back neck width A = 2E (straight part of front neck) + 2D (shaped part of front neck depth). There is no C as in fig. 1.

Sew in zip, following instructions, page 19.

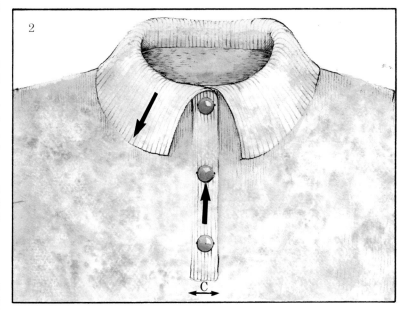

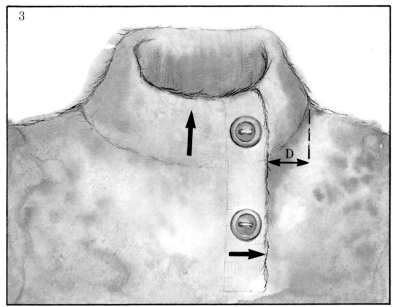

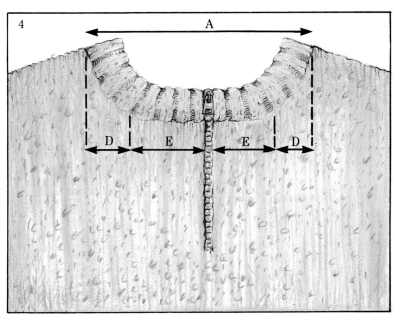

MATCHING FRONTS

Both sides of cardigan and jacket fronts must match exactly, the armhole, neck and shoulder shapings being in reverse. Each front may be knitted separately, or both at the same time to ensure a perfect match.

Stitches used for the main body of each half are normally half those required for the back, and front button bands (unless quite wide) are *added* to measurement. This extra width helps to keep the garment from 'gaping' in front when buttoned.

Both the front and back bodices are worked according to instructions on page 62–65, but the bodice front is worked in two identical halves, following the procedure described here.

Work each centre front edge straight until neck shaping begins, then work neck shaping according to chosen style, following instructions for neckline shapings given earlier in this chapter. See page 11 for attaching buttonhole band.

DOUBLE BREASTED STYLES

The width of each front (F in fig. 1), including button band, equals ½ back width + ½ overlap.

Shawl collar

In fig. 2 note that width of band (A) = back neck width, and F = ½ back minus ½A.

See instructions for shawl collar, page 82, and buttonholes, opposite.

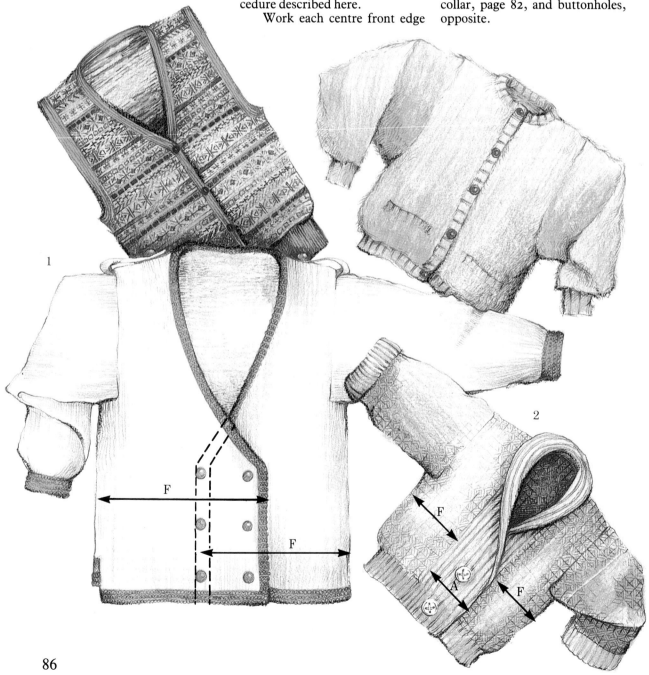

1

2

F

F

F

A

F

86

BUTTONHOLES

The correct spacing of buttonholes is most important to the appearance of finished garments. Mark the positions for buttons on the garment or button band, spacing the buttons evenly by measuring or by counting the stitches (or rows) along the length. Then make the buttonholes to correspond with button positions. Never put a button or a buttonhole at the very end of a piece of knitting; always place them *at least* 2 stitches from the ends.

Most buttonholes are improved by oversewing round them, or else by working round them in buttonhole stitch. Use either the same yarn as for garment, or use matching thread.

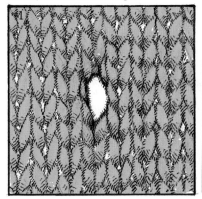

Round buttonholes

Although these are the easiest buttonholes to make, the style (fig. 1) is unfortunately only suitable for baby garments or for tiny buttons such as are sometimes used on evening wear.

At point where buttonhole is required, work as follows: K2tog, yrn/yo; continue working as before.

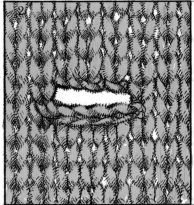

Horizontal buttonholes

This method (fig. 2) is usual to the type of buttonhole band made by picking up stitches along a side edge (button front, page 84), and

working a few rows. Keep in mind however that the buttonhole will be *vertical* in use.

It can also be worked directly into main fabric.

Horizontal buttonholes are made by casting/binding off 2 or more stitches in a row, and then casting on a corresponding number of stitches across the hole on the following row. This casting on can only be done by using the thumb method, and it leaves a loose stitch at beginning of cast-on stitches. To avoid this, work twice (page 14) into the last stitch before the buttonhole, and cast on one stitch less than required.

Alternatively, work into back of last stitch before buttonhole; cast on stitches required, and work into back of 1st stitch after buttonhole. This helps to make the cast-on stitches firmer.

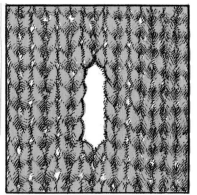

Vertical buttonholes

These (fig. 3) are useful for cardigan and other bands knitted lengthwise on a few stitches (example, page 84). The bands are sewn to the garment as work proceeds (page 11). Vertically *made*, these buttonholes will also be vertical in use.

Working
At the point where the buttonhole is required, ending wrong side row, divide the stitches in to two groups.

Work rows equal to buttonhole length on one group of the stitches, ending wrong side row, and leave these stitches on a holder or spare needle.

With another ball of yarn, work the same number of rows on 2nd group of stitches, ending wrong side row. Break off second ball.

Slip stitches from holder back on left-hand needle and continue work across all stitches.

POCKETS

A pocket top must be wide enough to allow the hand to enter easily. Its depth is usually at least the length of the fingers and more often the whole hand.

Patch pockets

These are the simplest pockets to make, consisting merely of a rectangle (fig. 1) sewn on to the knitted garment. The top edge (at least) must be in a stitch that will not curl, such as rib or garter stitch.

The pocket must be sewn on very neatly, preferably in the manner described below, the upper and lower edges being straight with the rows of knitting and the side edges parallel with a vertical line of stitches.

Attaching pockets
To mark a straight line of stitches, insert a fine knitting needle in the work, as shown in fig. 2, picking up alternate threads, and then slip

2

pocket   garment

stitch the pocket edge neatly to these threads, matching row for row if pocket is made at the same tension/gauge as main part.

The straight line of stitches to which the lower edge is joined may be worked in the same fashion.

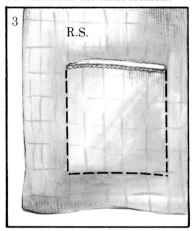

3   R.S.

Slit pocket

For this pocket (figs 3 and 4), a rectangle usually of st st stitch, is worked beforehand for the pocket lining (i.e. the pocket inside) and left on a holder.

When main part reaches length where pocket is required, proceed as follows, beginning with a right side row:
Next row: knit stitches in row up

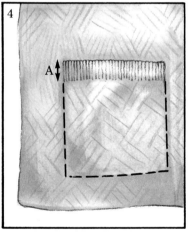

4

A

to position of pocket slit; cast/bind off stitches required for slit; work to end.
Following row: work back to slit, work pocket lining stitches on holder, work to end.

Note: to neaten the slit corners, work into back of last stitch before pocket lining stitches, and first stitch after them.
The lining is sewn down to inside of work after completion, following straight lines of stitches and rows as described for patch pockets.

1

Edged Slit

Fig. 4 shows a slit pocket where the top edge is worked in rib, as follows:

Next row: work across stitches to pocket slit, and slip stitches required for pocket top on to a holder. Work across stitches of pocket lining as described above, and complete row.

When bodice front is complete, return to the stitches on holder and work rib or other edge to depth required.

Sew down pocket lining to inside as described for patch pocket.

Sew down side edges (A) of pocket top edging.

Loose pocket

This is a double flap of fabric (fig. 5) formed while knitting the main part. It is not, however, suitable for heavyweight yarns – which tend to be too bulky – or to closely fitting garments.

At the position required for the pocket, and ending wrong side row, work stitches up to *and across* pocket width (B). Turn; work across pocket width stitches (B) again.

Continue on these stitches to twice the pocket depth required, and ending right side row. Work to edge.

Next row: turn; work across all stitches, to end of row.

Continue work on all stitches, tucking the double flap thus formed to inside.

After completion, join the side edges of the double flap.

RIBBING AND EDGINGS

Rib edges are usually worked on needles 2 or 3 sizes smaller than those used for main parts of the garment. This is because a rib stitch is more elastic and flexible than, say, st st. Rib edges will not curl, but to keep them flat they should be *slightly* stretched in relation to the rest of the garment.

The number of stitches required should be determined in the same way as for the main part of the garment (see Calculations, page 65). A separate tension/gauge square is necessary in the rib or edging of your choice.

TYPES OF RIB

Different rib patterns are best suited to different parts of a garment. A few examples are given here. (See also Stitch Library, page 24.)

K1 P1 rib is the simplest way to keep an edge flat, but it is not very elastic – suitable for collars and button bands.

K2 P2 rib is a satisfactory elastic ribbing which normally gives a much tighter tension/gauge than st st, thus obviating the need to make increases above it in many cases.

Other K P combinations such as K2 P1 or P3 K1, may also be used, particularly to 'run into' another stitch pattern above. However, with these as with twisted ribs, cable ribs and many others, there is a right and wrong side.

Pattern multiples

Since rib and many other edging patterns repeat over a fixed number of stitches – K2 P2 for instance over a multiple of 4 stitches – it may be necessary to adjust the total number of stitches in a neckline or cuff by increasing or decreasing in order to work the rib over the correct number of stitches. (Picking up neckline stitches, page 77.)

Decorative edgings

Any stitch which makes a flat, non-curling fabric can be used to make an edging, especially if it does not have to be elastic, e.g. garter stitch or moss stitch.

Fairisle patterns can be worked on a folded hem (page 75), or knitted as a long strip, folded lengthwise, and sewn round the edge of a garment. But this method can look rather bulky.

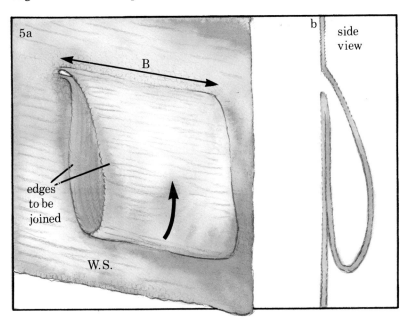

5a
B
edges to be joined
W.S.
b side view

COLOUR AND TEXTURE

Most of us are hesitant and uninspired when it comes to experimenting with colours and textures, and tend to shy away from creating patterns. Yet even a simple change of yarn and colour can produce the most unexpectedly brilliant effects. Discovering these capacities in different yarns, stitches, tones, and developing them by mixing colours, textures, or both, is a stimulating as well as therapeutic exercise. It also is a very productive one. But before you get carried away it is important to understand the composition of yarns and their qualities.

YARNS

For many people nothing replaces natural fibres: the elasticity and warmth of wool, the receptivity to colour of silk, the luxurious feel of angora and cashmere, and the cool crispness of linen and cotton. Yet it cannot be denied that man-made fibres and synthetic mixtures are on the whole inexpensive, easily cared for, and also provide a wealth of new surface textures.

Natural fibres

Wool is of course the chief material in the knitter's craft, but it requires special care if garments are to retain their shape and softness. Hand-washing or dry cleaning is essential in most cases, although some wool yarns are labelled superwash, which means they are machine washable providing the machine has a wool wash.

Lambswool, which comes from the first shearing is renowned for its warmth.

Botany wool is made from the fleece of the merino sheep and is extremely fine and soft. But most of the wool in standard knitting yarns is from a variety of breeds of sheep.

Mohair is the most commonly used animal fibre after wool. This is hair from the Angora goat. Strong and hardwearing, yet of a delicate appearance, it is often used to 'lighten' a texture that would otherwise be too solid: chunky tweeds for instance, or a thick cotton. Mohair is less elastic than wool, and more expensive. It is rarely available in its pure form, but often mixed with wool and acrylic. It can also be irritating to the skin because of its fluffy fibres. *Kid mohair* is softer, as it comes from the young animal, but it is even more expensive.

Angora is exceptionally fluffy with long, silky fibres. Although it looks and feels extremely luxurious, its fibres can irritate. Angora is obtained from the rabbit of the same name whose coat is combed regularly to procure the hair.

Cashmere is made from Cashmere goat hair and is rarely available as a knitting yarn. The fine soft quality is also light and warm, but extremely expensive. Cashmere is not hard-wearing and felts easily.

Alpaca is a soft and silky yarn spun from the coat of the llama. It can be used in its pure form or mixed with wool.

Silk, harvested from the silkworm – many hundreds of metres from a single cocoon – has been the premier thread ever since early Chinese dynasties made their royal robes from it. *Spun* *silk* is made by twisting together short fibres, and is usually coarser and cheaper, while smooth silk is often blended with other fibres, especially wool. It is very strong and durable, takes colour beautifully and 'glows'. One of the most expensive of yarns.

Cotton, the most sought after of knitting yarns, following wool and mohair, is now available in a glorious range of colours, textures and piles. Wonderfully cool to wear, but not as elastic as wool. *Mercerised cotton* has been treated to give it extra strength and lustre.

Linen, a heavy fibre produced from the stem of the flax plant and of ancient use is often blended with cotton or synthetic yarns. Its surface is slubbed.

Synthetic yarns

These are made from a variety of chemical components. The most familiar names are **polyester**, **nylon**, **rayon** and **acrylic**. These yarns are usually less expensive than natural fibres, and more practical since they wash and dry easily. They are also resistant to moth, do not felt and are strong and hard-wearing; but sometimes they lose their shape after several washes. Synthetic yarns are also light, which makes them very economical to use. The disadvantages of these yarns are mainly aesthetic, and even though over the years colour and texture have improved, the tactile qualities of natural fibres have not quite been matched. In addition, they do not keep the wearer either as warm or as cool as natural fibres like wool and cotton.

Novelty yarns are synthetic blends, usually representative of current fashion. They tend to stay in a range for one or two seasons only. Most of them are of an uneven texture and either boucléd, brushed or ragged.

Simulated suede, leather, ribbons, raffia and *latex* also come under this category.

Mixing yarns and stitches

Yarns may be mixed in several ways either by using different textured yarns, like chenille, silk, tweed and cotton, or by combining finer yarns and knitting them as one to get more variation in tone or finish. For instance, if you use a chunky tweed yarn, you could combine it with a mohair and wool; or a fine chenille with cotton of double knitting/worsted thickness. But it is very important to keep the *overall* thickness more or less even. In each knitted piece the tension/gauge must be uniform, but it can change in other pieces which are sewn on separately.

You can create different effects too by mixing stitch patterns and colour. The photograph overleaf shows some of the combinations that are feasible. Go one step further: use knitting as pure art form and experiment with sequins, beads, silk strips, ribbons, feather, fur and embroidery to build up interesting surface detail. This added dimension can be very effective and turn an otherwise plain style into something genuinely outstanding and unique.

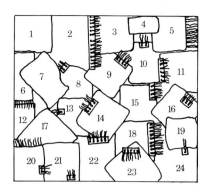

Key to types of yarns used for swatches opposite. In general these yarns have been kept to standard DK/worsted weights.

1 Viscose/lurex, wool, mohair, raw silk, angora and feathers – 5mm (UK6 US8) needles. 2 Strips of silk fabric and viscose – 5½mm (UK5 US9) needles. 3 Silk, viscose, kid mohair and angora – 4mm (UK8 US5–6) needles. 4 Silk and viscose – 4mm (UK8 US5–6) needles. 5 Lurex, Angora, mohair, silk and viscose – 4mm (UK8 US5–6) needles. 6 Mohair and silk – 5½mm (UK6 US9) needles. 7 Angora, tweedy cotton plain cotton, sequinned thread – 4mm (UK8 US5 –6) needles. 8 Polyamide – 4mm (UK8 US5–6) needles. 9 Pure wool DK/worsted 4½mm (UK7 US7) needles. 10 Wool DK, multicoloured cotton blend – 4½mm (UK7 US7) needles. 11 Kid mohair, silk, angora and lurex – 4½mm (UK7 US7) needles. 12 Mohair, silk, angora, cotton, viscose – 4mm (UK8 US5–6) needles. 13 Polyamide 4mm (UK8 US5–6) needles. 14 Mohair – 5½mm (UK5 US9) needles. 15 Pure wool – 4½ mm (UK7 US7) needles. 16 Wool blend tweed, plain wool – 5½mm (UK5 US9) needles. 17 Viscose, metalized Polyester, viscose/wool/nylon, mohair/wool/nylon – 5½mm (UK5 US9) needles. 18 Angora, viscose, mohair, cotton, wool, ribbons, beads – 5½mm (UK5 US9) needles. 19 Pure silk – 4½ mm (UK7 US7) needles. 20 Mohair blends – 4mm (UK8 US5–6) needles. 21 Silk, angora – 4½mm (UK7 US7) needles. 22 Angora, Kid mohair, silk, viscose, fur – 5mm (UK6 US8) needles. 23 Mohair blend, silk lurex, angora, beads – 5mm (UK6 US8) needles. 24 Angora/wool blend – 4½mm (UK7 US7) needles.

MULTI-COLOUR DESIGN

Generally speaking, the decorative patterns on knitwear are of two types: small repeating motifs such as fairisle patterns in which yarn for each colour is carried across the back of the work, and larger, single motifs such as pictures or random repeats worked by the intarsia method (using different balls of yarn for each area of colour). Both are plotted on graph paper where each square equals 1 stitch. The methods for working are described below.

A third form of decoration, usually for a very small motif or part of a larger one, is Swiss darning/duplicate stitch, applied after knitting is complete (see page 17).

REPEATING PATTERNS

In small repeating patterns such as fairisle, where yarn is carried across the back of the work, the number of stitches to 4″ is usually more or less equal to the number of rows to 4″. In other words, the stitches and rows are the same in each direction (fig. 1). This is because carrying yarn across the back of the fabric actually distorts the tension/gauge, and it makes designing the repeat comparatively easy.

Plotting a design

To correctly fit a repeating band across the garment, you must first convert the garment measurements into stitches and rows (following formulae on page 65), and find out how many times the motif will repeat across the work. You must decide too upon the width of the gap between the repeats.

If the pattern repeat does not fit easily into the stitches available, work a few background stitches at each edge or make the gap between the motifs 1 or 2 stitches wider.

Following the instructions opposite for using graph paper, lightly sketch in the outline of your motif. If it needs to be enlarged (or reduced), see Enlarging, overleaf.

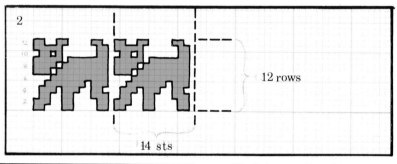

Work in pencil at this stage so that you can make changes easily, and remember to include the gap between the motifs as part of the chart, e.g. fig. 2. In this diagram, the dog is 13 sts wide with a gap of 1 st, so the pattern repeats over 14 sts. (The gap could be 2 or more sts if required.)

Overdraw the outline, taking each line to the nearest little square and making the diagonal lines run in smooth, even 'steps'.

When satisfied with the design, use crayons to lightly colour it in so that you can count the squares underneath.

Working

Work according to the two-colour method.

To read the chart: read right side (odd number) knit rows from right to left and wrong side (even number) purl rows from left to right.

TWO COLOUR KNITTING

When knitting a *row* with two colours, the colour not in use needs to be carried across the back of the work to the point where it is next required. There are several ways of doing this, depending on how the yarn is held in the fingers; some people work with the second colour in the left hand; some work with both yarns in the right hand, over the first and second fingers. Whatever method of holding is used, there are two basic ways of carrying the yarns, and practice will show which way is easier for you.

With any of the methods given below, both colours should always be taken to the very end of every row and twisted together at the beginning of the next row (unless a new colour is being introduced), otherwise the edge of the work will be uneven and loose.

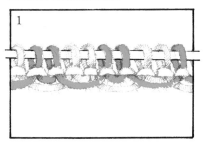

Stranding. The yarns are carried across the back of the work without twisting, with one colour always above the other (fig. 1). This method is best where up to four stitches occur in each colour. Care should be taken not to pull too tightly or the work will pucker.

Weaving. The colour not in use is 'woven' into the back of the fabric by carrying it above the colour in use for one stitch, and below it for the next (fig. 2). In this way, a colour may be carried across large groups of stitches without forming 'floats' or big loops on the back of the fabric, but again care must be taken not to pull tightly or the tension/gauge will be affected.

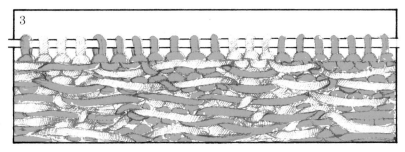

Stranding/weaving combination (fig. 3). This is a useful technique combining both the previous methods. Strand the colours when passing across, say, up to four stitches; to pass behind larger groups of stitches, twist the yarns every two or three stitches at the back of the work to avoid long 'floats'. Stagger the position of the twists from row to row to avoid showing on right side of work.

USING GRAPH PAPER

Graph paper is a sheet covered with a grid of squares. It is used in knitting as an aid to counting stitches in a stitch or colour pattern, or to plot diagonal lines or curves, e.g. batwing and raglan sleeves.

Graph paper with 8 or 10 squares per inch is the best size for general use. Some knitting shops sell specialist graph paper in which the squares are widened to correspond with the actual shape of the knitted stitch. This is easier to work with and is available in several grid sizes.

Plotting

Before you begin to mark or colour the squares, you must know how many stitches/rows make up your required measurement. (See conversion formulae, page 65.)

Draw the outline of the piece on graph paper so each square equals one stitch.

Diagonal and curved lines must always be drawn in 'steps' (figs. A and B). These mimic the increases and decreases typical of knitwear shaping. Diagonal lines progress in a steady stairstep, but curves are plotted in groups of stitches which vary in size (see Batwing sleeves, page 69). The steeper the angle required, the 'taller' the step must be.

Number rows vertically up the side of the graph (see example overleaf). Stitches may be numbered along lower edge if required.

Textural patterns are sometimes marked stitch by stitch in the squares (fig. C).

In multi-coloured work it is useful to colour each area to approximate that of the finished design. Use crayons or coloured pencils, but keep to lighter hues so that the squares underneath may be counted easily.

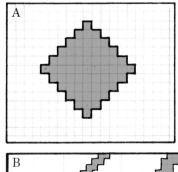

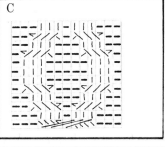

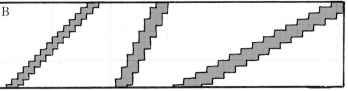

Large motifs are normally worked in stocking/stockinette stitch using the intarsia method which is described overleaf. But before you begin, the motif must first be plotted on graph paper and probably enlarged in size so that it fits the required area. Therefore, you need to know the measurement the motif will be on the garment itself and the tension/gauge which you will be using to knit it.

Follow the conversion formulae on page 65 and convert the desired measurements into stitches and rows.

Enlarging a motif

If you are copying a motif, for example, something in a book or magazine, it will probably need to be enlarged. The following method can also be used in reverse to reduce size.

Place a sheet of tracing paper over the motif and trace the main lines with a pencil. Then, using a ruler, divide the tracing into 1″ squares as shown in fig. 1.

By comparing the original size of the motif with the size you want it to be, you will discover how many times you will need to enlarge it. For example, if the motif in fig. 1 is 3″ × 4″ and you want to make it 9″ × 12″, it will have to be enlarged to 3 times its present size.

Draw a rectangle the size you wish the motif to be (in our example 9″ × 12″) and divide it into the same number of squares as the tracing (fig. 2). (In our example each square will be 3″ × 3″.)

Copy the lines within each of the 1″ squares into the corresponding larger squares. (If your design is complicated, you could make smaller squares within each new square so it will be easier to follow the outline.)

Check that the design is now the size you want.

Plotting the design

Take a sheet of graph paper (8 or 10 squares per inch), or use specialist graph paper. Then, with a pencil, draw a rectangle representing the size of the area you wish the design to fill, so that 1 square equals 1 stitch.

Divide the rectangle into smaller rectangles corresponding with the squares on the enlarged design, i.e. dotted lines in fig. 3.

If you are working with ordinary graph paper, your design will look distorted and appear much taller than in the original. This is because *knitted* stitches are wider than they are long, and are not square like the graph paper. Don't worry: it will come right again in the knitting.

Still using pencil, copy lightly the lines of your drawing on to the graph, making the lines within each square fit within each corresponding rectangle, as shown.

Redraw each line following the line of the nearest square. In the case of a symmetrical motif or area, such as the *fleur de lys* shown, adjust the outline so that it is the same on both sides; adjust diagonal lines to make evenly stepped slopes.

When you are happy with the design, redraw the outlines with a fine felt tipped pen and erase the pencil marks.

Colour the design lightly so that you can still see the squares to count them.

Working

Work in intarsia as described overleaf.
Read the chart as follows: read right side (odd number) knit rows from right to left and wrong side (even number) purl rows from left to right.

Small areas of 2 or 3 stitches may be Swiss darned/duplicate stitched after knitting is complete.

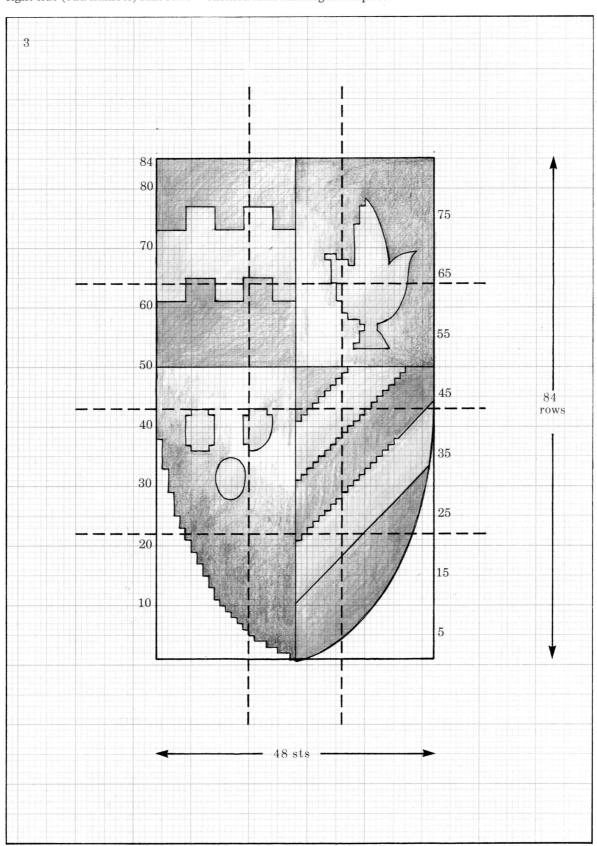

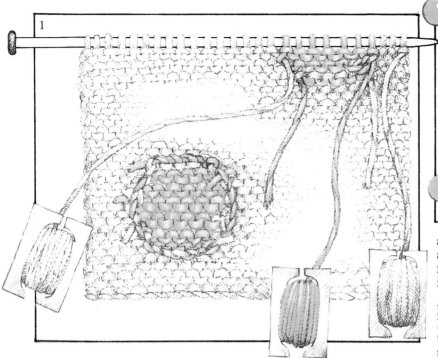

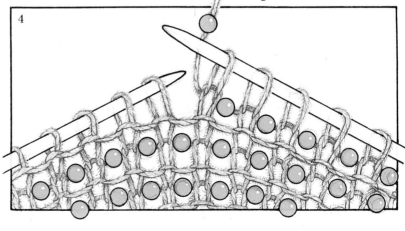

and every alternate row (fig. 4), to avoid curling, omit beads from first and last stitches on row. Work in garter stitch throughout.

Beaded areas
Beaded fabric can be rather solid; therefore it is often preferable to space the beads or sequins out, or else concentrate them in a small area.

Place threaded bead on right side rows of st st as follows and at point required, bring yarn forward between needles; slip next stitch; push bead up yarn close to right-hand needle; return yarn to back between needles and K next stitch. Bead is thus held in front of slipped stitch.

EMBROIDERY

Use either the same knitting yarn as you are working on, or choose embroidery silks of the same thickness. Swiss darning/duplicate stitch (see page 17), is the most commonly used form of embroidery since it imitates knitting and is quick to apply. You can also use this stitch to correct mistakes.
Cross stitch, smocking or **basic embroidery** stitches look wonderful on a traditional peasant knitwear design.

INTARSIA

This method is used in non-repeating multi-coloured patterns, particularly where large areas of several different colours occur, such as a pictorial motif or abstract design.
To work a coloured motif in intarsia, a separate ball of yarn must be used for each area of colour (fig. 1). Yarn must never be passed across the back of the work from one area to another, even by a few stitches; it may be very tempting but the result will be a puckered piece of knitting which you will be unable to flatten no matter how hard you try.
Bobbins. In order to keep the several different balls of yarn from tangling, wind each strand on to a bobbin cut out of stiff card (fig. 2). (You can buy ready-made bobbins in good knitting shops.) Chunky/bulky yarns will require a larger bobbin than the one illustrated. Pass the working end through the narrow slot as shown.

Keep all the bobbins on the wrong side of the work.
Changing colours on a row. To prevent a gap between two areas of colour, twist the yarns one over the other on the wrong side of the work.

BEADS

Beads are often threaded on to the yarn before you begin knitting; so are sequins. Make sure that the beads are not too heavy for the yarn and remember that holes must be big enough to be threaded on yarn.
To thread, attach the yarn to a loop of ordinary sewing cotton which has been threaded on the needle (fig. 3).

Beaded fabric
Introduce beads from the back of the knitting, slipping one bead between each stitch on the second

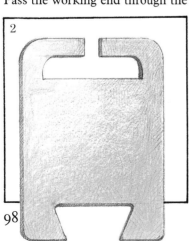

STEP-BY-STEP PATTERNS

The following patterns are for the sweaters illustrated on pages 34–59.

In addition to step-by-step instructions, each pattern contains a diagram of the sweater parts. The letters on the diagram are keyed to measurements in the accompanying 'box'. Yarn and needles required to knit the pattern are also stated in the 'box'.

To find out how to read a knitting pattern, see page 15. A list of knitting abbreviations appears in the front endpapers.

Remember that it is always necessary to check tension/gauge before commencing (see page 12). If you need smaller or larger needles to obtain correct tension/gauge for the main parts, you should use correspondingly smaller or larger needles for the ribbing or edging.

Read through the pattern before you begin and check out anything which you do not understand. The stitches, and most of the stitch patterns, are explained at the top of the patterns. But where there is a stitch chart, each marked square represents one stitch (see page 94 for details).

ADAPTING PATTERNS

The patterns are organised so that they can be adapted to suit individual tastes and requirements. This means they can be knitted in a different yarn or stitch from that which is designated, or changed in shape (bodice or sleeves made longer or shorter, necklines restyled).

To facilitate this, each pattern contains *in italics* a brief description of what is actually going on at each stage as you follow the step-by-step instructions. In addition, measurements for each size are given over all parts of the garment.

Before altering a pattern it is important to read Adapting pattern measurements (page 20) and to become familiar with relevant sections of the tailoring chapter, most particularly the formulae for converting measurements into stitches and rows (Essential calculations, page 65), which is crucial to calculating all changes in stitch type or tension/gauge.

Yarn substitution

If using yarn which is *equivalent* to the yarn prescribed, it is wise to buy one ball first in order to check the tension/gauge. If it does *not* match that of the pattern, do not change needles by more than 2 or 3 sizes or the resulting fabric will be either too floppy or too stiff. The alternative is to use the diagram and measurements as described to calculate your own stitches and rows, and re-calculate any increases or decreases (using graph paper if in doubt – page 95).

The front endpapers contain a guide to average yarn requirements for sweaters knitted in st st with different types of yarn. For calculating yarn requirements more precisely, see page 16.

Stitch substitution

Again, check your tension/gauge first and make any necessary changes in required numbers of stitches and rows, as explained above.

If the stitch pattern you are using has a stitch multiple, e.g. K2 P2 (a multiple of 4 sts), you will of course have to adjust the overall number of stitches accordingly, so that the stitch pattern comes out evenly. If, however, the adjustment is more than 2 or 3 stitches, re-calculate the width of the stitches to ensure you will be happy with the result.

Note that the measurements and the materials required to knit each pattern appear in a ruled box, as does the diagram of pattern pieces.

The pattern itself begins with the tension/gauge, in other words, where you begin to knit.

SAILOR STRIPES

TENSION/GAUGE

22 sts and 28 rows = 4″ measured over st st using lge needles.

STITCHES USED

garter stitch (g st) – all rows K.

Stripe pattern:
12 rows st st in col B, 12 rows st st in col A. Rep 24 rows.

MAIN PIECE

Begin at lower front edge.
Using sm needles and col A cast on 76(82, 90, 100, 104, 110, 116, 120, 126) sts *to give measurement A at st st tension.*

Work in g st for 1½″ ending odd no of rows for neater lower edge (approx 17 rows).
Change to lge needles and work in stripe pattern as above to length F ending 6th row of stripe.

Shape sleeves

Cast on 25(30, 40, 50, 52, 55, 58, 60, 63) sts at beg next 2 rows *measurement C, less cuff,* at each side. 126(142, 170, 200, 208, 220, 232, 240, 252) sts *twice B, less cuffs.* Work to length E ending 6th row of a stripe.

Shape neck

next row: K 40(46, 60, 74, 76, 82, 87, 91, 96) sts. Cast off next 46(50, 50, 52, 56, 56, 58, 58, 60) sts *measurement D;* work to end.
foll row: P, casting on 46(50, 50, 52, 56, 56, 58, 58, 60) sts over neck opening.
Complete the back half in reverse, matching stripes and sleeve shaping.

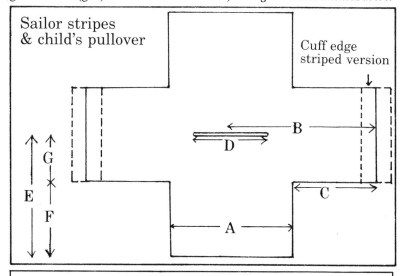

Sailor stripes & child's pullover

Cuff edge striped version

B

D

G

E

F

C

A

MEASUREMENTS REFER TO DIAGRAM (*measurements in inches*)

to fit bust/chest	24	26	28	30	32	34	36	38	40
actual measurement (twice A)	28	30	33	36	38	40	42	44	46
Width across chest (A)	14	15	16½	18	19	20	21	22	23
centre back neck to folded cuff edge (B)	13	14½	17	19½	20½	21½	22½	23½	24½
sleeve seam (cuff folded) (C)	6	7	8¾	10½	11	11½	12	12½	13
neck opening width (D)	8½	9	9	9½	10	10	10½	10½	11
length to shoulder (E)	14¼	17¾	20¼	23¼	24¾	26¼	26¼	27¾	27¾
length below sleeve (F)	9¾	11¼	12¾	15¾	15¾	15¾	15¾	17¼	17¼
half sleeve depth (G)	4½	6¼	7½	7½	9¼	10½	10½	10½	10½

Note: twice B = A plus twice C.

MATERIALS

Emu Superwash DK/worsted (Standard DK/worsted wool)

col A cream – gms	200	200	250	250	300	300	350	350	350
col B navy – gms	150	150	200	200	250	250	300	300	300

Needles for main part (lge): 4mm (UK 8, US 5–6)
Needles for edging (sm): 3¼mm (UK 10, US 3)

CUFFS

With right side of sleeve facing using sm. needles and col A pick up and K 50(66, 84, 84, 102, 120, 120, 120, 120) sts evenly from sleeve edge, *twice G.*
Work in g st for 3″ ending even no of rows. Cast off.

TO MAKE UP

Join underarm and side seams matching stripes leaving g st rows open at lower edges to form side splits.
Press according to ball bands omitting g st.
Fold cuffs back. Allow neck edge to roll.

CHILD'S PULLOVER

TENSION/GAUGE

21 sts and 38 rows = 4″ measured over g st using lge needles.

STITCHES USED

g st (garter stitch) – all rows K.

MEASUREMENTS REFER TO DIAGRAM (measurements in inches)

to fit bust/chest	24	26	28	30	32	34	36	38	40
actual measurement (twice A)	28	30	33	36	38	40	42	44	46
width across chest (A)	14	15	16½	18	19	20	21	22	23
centre back neck to sleeve edge (B)	17½	19½	21¼	23	24½	26	27½	28½	29
sleeve seam (C)	10½	12	13	14	15	16	17	17½	18
neck opening width (D)	8½	9	9	9½	10	10	10½	10½	11
length to shoulder (E)	14½	17	20	23	25	26	26½	27	27½
length below sleeve (F)	10	11	12½	15½	16	16	16	16½	17
half sleeve depth (G)	4½	6	7½	7½	9	10	10½	10½	10½

Note: centre back neck to sleeve edge (B) = ½ width across chest (A) + sleeve seam (C). Length to shoulder (E) = length below sleeve (F) + half sleeve depth (G).

MATERIALS

Pingouin Confort: (Standard DK/worsted yarn)

col A navy – gms	250	250	250	300	300	350	350	400	400
col B ecru – gms	50	50	50	100	100	100	100	150	150

Needles for main parts (lge): 4mm (UK 8, US 5–6)

Needles for lower edges (sm): 3¼mm (UK 10, US 3)

2 buttons if required

MAIN PIECE

Begin at lower front edge.

Using sm needles and col A cast on 74(78, 86, 94, 100, 104, 110, 114, 120) sts – *measurement A at main tension*.

Work in g st for 1½″ ending w s row.

Change to lge needles.

Cont in g st to length F minus 3″ ending w s row.

Change to col B. Cont to length F ending w s row.

Shape Sleeves

Change to col A. Cast on 54(62, 68, 74, 80, 84, 88, 92, 96) sts at beg next 2 rows (*measurement C*).

Total 182(202, 222, 242, 260, 272, 286, 298, 312) sts – *twice measurement B*.

Cont to length E ending w s row.

Shape neck

next row: K 69(77, 87, 96, 104, 110, 115, 121, 127) sts, cast off next 44(48, 48, 50, 52, 52, 56, 56, 58) sts (*measurement D*); K to end.

foll row: K, casting on 44(48, 48, 50, 52, 52, 56, 56, 58) sts over neck opening.

Complete the back half in reverse matching sleeve shapings and stripes.

TO MAKE UP

Join side and sleeve seams.

Fasten neck edge with a button and loop at each side if required.

Press according to instructions on ball bands.

TWO STITCHES

(Measurements and materials overleaf.)

TENSION/GAUGE

17 sts and 24 rows = 4″ measured over st st using lge needles.

STITCHES USED

st st.

rev st st – purl side is r s.

g st – all rows K.

K1 P2 rib – multiple of 3 sts.
  row 1: K1 *K1 P2* repeat * to * to last 2 sts, K2.
  row 2: K1 *P1 K2* repeat * to * to last 2 sts, P1, K1.
  Repeat 2 rows.

MAIN PIECE

Begin at lower front edge.

Using sm needles cast on 75(78, 81, 87, 90, 93) sts *to give measurement A at st st tension, adjusted to multiple of 3 for ribbing*.

Work in K1 P2 rib for 2″ ending w s row and inc 3(4, 5, 3, 4, 5) sts evenly across last row. 78(82, 86, 90, 94, 98) sts *measurement A at st st tension*.

Change to lge needles.

1st row: K 39(41, 43, 45, 47, 49) sts *to centre*, P to last st, K1.

2nd row: as 1st row.

Repeat these 2 rows to length F ending w s row.

Shape sleeves

Keeping reverse stitch pattern in position as set, cast on 3 sts at beg next 40(40, 42, 42, 44, 44) rows and 4(6, 5, 7, 6, 8) sts at beg foll 2 rows, *thus adding measurement C at each side*.

206(214, 222, 230, 238, 246) sts – *twice measurement B*.

Work to length E minus H ending w s row.

Shape Neck

Left side

next row: K 93(97, 100, 104, 107, 111) sts, turn. Work on these sts only.

2nd row: cast off 3 sts, work to end.

3rd row: work to end. Repeat these 2 rows once more.

6th row: P2tog, work to end.

7th row: Work to last 2 sts, K2tog.

8th row: as 6th.

84(88, 91, 95, 98, 102) sts rem – *measurement B, half D*.

Work to length E ending w s row.

Slip sts to holder.

Right side

With right side of work facing slip 20(20, 22, 22, 24, 24) sts at centre to holder. Rejoin yarn and complete row.

Work 1 w s row.

Shape to match left side, working neck edge decs as skpo on r s rows and P2tog, tbl on w s rows.
Work to length E ending w s row.

Back of neck
Cast on (2 needle method) 38(38, 40, 40, 42, 42) sts across back of neck, *measurement D*.

Back

With right side facing, work across left side sts on holder, back neck sts and right side sts, changing pattern at centre back. 206(214, 222, 230, 238, 246) sts.
Work to length E plus ½ J ending w s row.

Shape sleeve

Cast off 4(6, 5, 7, 6, 8) sts at beg next 2 rows, 3 sts at beg foll 40(40, 42, 42, 44, 44) rows. 78(82, 86, 90, 94, 98) sts rem.
Complete the back matching length to front.

NECK EDGE

With right side facing using set of 4 dp or circular sm needles, pick up and K 82(82, 86, 86, 90, 90) sts from neck edge.
round 1: P.
Cast off.

CUFFS

With right side facing using sm needles pick up and K 36 sts from sleeve edge.
Beg rib row 2, work 1″ of K1 P2 rib, ending rib row 2. Cast off in rib.

TO MAKE UP

Join side and sleeve seams.
Press according to instructions on ballbands.

RIBBON TOP

(Measurements, materials, overleaf.)

TENSION/GAUGE

22 sts and 28 rows = 4″ measured over st st using lge needles.
Note: because of the unusual nature of this yarn, a standard DK/worsted tension gauge is produced with much larger needles than usual. If substituting yarn, check needle size carefully.

STITCHES USED

st st.
g st – all rows K.
K2 P2 rib – multiple of 4 sts.
    row 1: K1 *K2 P2 rep from * to last 3 sts, K3.
    row 2: K1 *P2 K2 rep from * to last 3 sts, P2, K1.
    Repeat 2 rows.

FRONT AND BACK

Front and back are alike.
Using sm needles cast on 96(100, 104, 108, 116) sts – *measurement A at st st tension, less allowance to tighten rib.*
Work in K2 P2 rib for 3″ ending rib row 1.

Two stitches

D   B   1″   J

H

G

E

Rev.St.St.   St. St.   C

F

A

MEASUREMENTS REFER TO SAILOR STRIPES DIAGRAM
(*measurements in inches*)

to fit bust/chest	30	32	34	36	38	40
actual measurement (twice measurement A)	36	38	40	42	44	46
width across chest (A)	18	19	20	21	22	23
centre back neck to top of cuff (B)	24	25	26	27	28	29
sleeve seam (C)	15	15½	16	16½	17	17½
neck opening width (D)	9	9	9½	9½	10	10
length to shoulder (E)	26	26½	27	27½	28	28½
length below sleeve (F)	14	14½	14½	15	15	15½
depth at armhole (G)	12	12	12½	12½	13	13
neck opening depth (H)	2	2	2	2	2	2
cuff width (J)	8½	8½	8½	8½	8½	8½

MATERIALS

Wendy Fiori (Aran/sport weight cotton – gms	500	550	550	600	600	650

Needles for main part (lge): 5mm (UK 6, US 8)
Needles for edgings (sm): 4mm (UK 8, US 5–6)
Double-ended (dp) or circular sm needles: 4mm (UK 8, US 5–6)

Inc 4(4, 6, 6, 4) sts evenly across next rib row. 100(104, 110, 114, 120) sts – *to give measurement A at st st tension.*
Change to lge needles. Work in st st to length F ending w s row.

Shape sleeves

Cast on 6 sts (*measurement C*) at beg next 2 rows. 112(116, 122, 126, 132) sts – *twice measurement B.*
Work to length E ending w s row.
Cast off 31(33, 33, 35, 36) sts at beg next 2 rows. 50(50, 56, 56, 60) sts

rem – *measurement D.*
Change to sm needles. Work 2 rows g st. Cast off.

SLEEVE EDGES

Join shoulder seams. With right side facing using sm needles pick up and K 80 sts evenly from sleeve edge. Work 1 row g st. Cast off.

TO MAKE UP

Join side seams. Press according to instructions on ball bands.

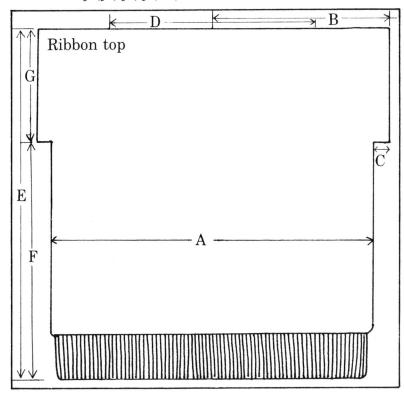

Ribbon top

MEASUREMENTS REFER TO DIAGRAM (*measurements in inches*)

to fit bust	32	34	36	38	40
actual measurement (twice measurement A)	36	38	40	42	44
width across bust (A)	18	19	20	21	22
centre back neck to sleeve edge (B)	10	10½	11	11½	12
sleeve extension (C)	1	1	1	1	1
neck opening width (D)	9	9	10	10	11
length to shoulder (E)	21	21	21½	21½	22
length below sleeve (F)	11½	11½	12	12	12½
half sleeve depth (G)	9½	9½	9½	9½	9½
MATERIALS					
Avocet Soirée – gms col Pewter 509	450	450	450	500	500

Needles for main part (lge): 5½mm (UK 5, US 9)
Needles for edging (sm): 4½mm (UK 7, US 7)

MOHAIR COWL
(Measurements and materials, overleaf.)

TENSION/GAUGE

15 sts and 22 rows = 4″ measured over st st using lge needles.

STITCHES USED

K2 P2 rib:
 w s rows: K1, *K2 P2 rep from * to last 3 sts, K3.
 r s rows: K1, *P2 K2 rep from * to last 3 sts, P2, K1.
st st

BACK

Using sm needles and col A, cast on 60(64, 68, 72, 76, 80) sts – *measurement A less allowance to tighten rib.*
Work in K2, P2 rib to length F ending w s row.
Change to lge needles and col B.
next row: K 0(2, 4, 6, 3, 5), *K tw, K 5(5, 5, 5, 6, 6) rep from * to last 0(2, 4, 6, 3, 5) sts, K 0(2, 4, 6, 3, 5). 70(74, 78, 82, 86, 90) sts – *measurement A at st st tension.*
foll row: K1, P to last st, K1.
Work all wrong side rows of st st in this way for a neat edge.
Work 8 more rows st st (10 rows in all ending P row).
Change to col A. Cont in st st to length G ending w s row. Mark each end next row with a contrast thread. ★★
Cont in st st to length E ending w s row.

Shape shoulders

Cast off 7(7, 8, 8, 9, 9) sts at beg next 4 rows.
Cast off 6(8, 7, 9, 8, 10) sts at beg foll 2 rows.
Hold rem 30(30, 32, 32, 34, 34) sts – *measurement C* – on a holder.

FRONT

Work as back to ★★.
Cont in st st to length E minus K ending w s row.

Shape neck 1st side

next row: K 24(26, 27, 29, 30, 32) sts, turn. Work on these sts only.
2nd row: P2tog, work to end.
3rd row: work to last 2 sts, K2tog.
Repeat 2nd and 3rd rows once more. 20(22, 23, 25, 26, 28) sts

rem – *measurement D*.
Work 1 w s row.

row.
Cast off rem 6(8, 7, 9, 8, 10) sts.

Shape shoulder

Cast off 7(7, 8, 8, 9, 9) sts at beg next and foll alt row. Work 1 w s

2nd side

With r s of front facing, slip 22(22, 24, 24, 26, 26) sts at centre to a

holder and rejoin col A at right of rem sts.
Complete the row. Complete to match 1st side, reversing shaping by working neck edge decs as 'P2tog tbl' on P rows and as 'sl 1, K1, psso' on K rows.

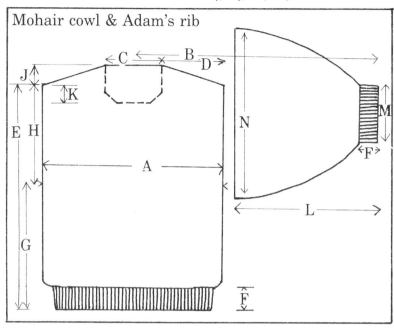

Mohair cowl & Adam's rib

MEASUREMENTS REFER TO DIAGRAM (*measurements in inches*)

to fit chest	30	32	34	36	38	40
actual measurement (= twice A)	37	39	41	43½	46	48
chest width (A)	18½	19½	20½	21½	23	24
centre back neck to cuff (B)	25	25½	26½	27	28	28½
back neck width (C)	8	8	8½	8½	9	9
each shoulder width (D)	5¼	5¾	6	6½	7	7½
length to shoulder (E)	26	26½	27	27½	28	28½
welt and cuff depth (F)	3	3	3	3	3	3
body length to underarm (G)	16½	17	17	17½	17½	18
armhole depth (H)	9½	9½	10	10	10½	10½
shoulder shaping depth (J)	1	1	1	1	1	1
front neck shaping depth (K)	1	1	1	1	1	1
sleeve seam length (L)	16	16	16½	16½	17	17
sleeve width at cuff (M)	8½	8½	9	9	9½	9½
sleeve width at top (N)	19½	19½	20½	20½	21½	21½

Note: centre back neck to cuff measurement (B) = ½ chest width (A) + sleeve seam length (L). Length to shoulder (E) = body length to underarm (G) + armhole depth (H).

MATERIALS

Argyll Finesse (knits as standard mohair)

col A Purple 145 – gms	450	450	450	500	500	500
col B Gold 178 – gms	75	75	75	75	75	75

Needles for main part (lge): 5½mm (UK 5, US 9)
Needles for ribbing (sm): 4½mm (UK 7, US 7)
Set of 4 double-ended (dp) or circular sm needles

SLEEVES

Using sm needles and col A cast on 36(36, 40, 40, 44, 44) sts – *measurement M* – and work in K2, P2 rib to length F ending w s row.
Change to lge needles.
next row: K 2(2, 4, 4, 2, 2), *K tw, K 7(7, 7, 7, 9, 9) rep from * to last 2(2, 4, 4, 2, 2) sts, K to end.
40(40, 44, 44, 48, 48) sts.
Work in st st beg with a P row, and inc 1 st at each end next r s row and every foll 4th row until there are 74(74, 78, 78, 82, 82) sts – *measurement N*.
Work without shaping to length L minus 10 rows ending w s row (adjust sleeve length here if required).
Change to col B. Work 10 rows st st.
Cast off in col B.

NECKBAND

Join shoulder seams.
Using dp or circ sm needle and col A, K up 30(30, 32, 32, 34, 34) sts from back of neck; pick up and K 8 sts from 1st side neck shaping; K up 22(22, 24, 24, 26, 26) sts from centre front and pick up and K 8 sts from 2nd side neck shaping. 68(68, 72, 72, 76, 76) sts.
round 1: *K2, P2 rep from * to end.
Repeat this round to length 2" ending at same point as start.
Change to a lge needle and cast off in rib as set.

TO MAKE UP

Join top edges of sleeves to armhole edges between marking threads. Join side and sleeve seams.
Fold neckband in half to inside and sew down neatly ensuring an easy fit over head.
Press according to instructions on ball bands.
Brush lightly with a teazle brush to raise the pile on mohair if required.

COWL

One size: to fit average head: circumference 32" depth 16".

Using dp or circ sm needle(s) and col A cast on 120 sts and join into a circle without twisting.

round 1: *K2, P2 rep from * to end.

Repeat this round until piece measures 1″ ending at same point as start.

Change to lge needle(s) and work in st st (all rounds K) to length 13″ ending at same point as start.

Change to col B and work 10 rounds st st ending at same point as start.

Change to col A. K1 round.

Change to sm needle(s) and work in rib as lower edge for 1″ ending at same point as start.

Change to a lge needle and cast off in rib as set.

ADAM'S RIB

TENSION/GAUGE

24 sts and 34 rows = 4″ over broken rib below using lge needles.

STITCHES USED

K1 P2 rib – multiple of 3 sts:
  r s rows: K1, *K1 P2 rep from * to last 2 sts, K2.
  w s rows: K1, *P1 K2 rep from * to last 2 sts, P1, K1.
Broken rib – multiple of 6 sts, plus 5:
  r s rows: *K5, P1 rep from * to last 5 sts, K5.
  w s rows: K2, *P1, K5 rep from * to last 3 sts, P1, K2.

BACK

Using sm needles cast on 99(105, 111, 117, 123, 129) sts.

Work in K1, P2 rib to length F, ending r s row.

inc row: rib 4(3, 3, 2, 2, 5), *wk tw, rib 12(13, 14, 15, 16, 16) rep from * to last 4(4, 3, 3, 2, 5) sts, wk tw, rib 3(3, 2, 2, 1, 4).
107(113, 119, 125, 131, 137) sts – *measurement A at main tension.*

Change to lge needles.

Work in broken rib to length G ending w s row.

Mark each end next row with a contrast thread. **

Work without shaping to length E, ending w s row.

Shape shoulders

Keeping pattern constant, cast off 9(9, 10, 10, 11, 11) sts at beg next 6 rows.

Cast off 8(10, 9, 11, 10, 12) sts at beg next 2 rows.

Slip rem 37(39, 41, 43, 45, 47) sts onto a holder – *measurement C.*

FRONT

Work as back to **.

Work to length E minus K ending w s row.

Shape neck 1st side

next row: work 41(43, 45, 47, 49, 51) sts, turn.

Work on these sts only. Keeping pattern constant throughout, shape as follows.

2nd row: P2tog, work to end.
3rd row: work to last 2 sts, K2tog.
4th row: as 2nd.
5th row: work in patt.
6th row: as 2nd.

Repeat 5th and 6th rows twice more. 35(37, 39, 41, 43, 45) sts rem – *measurement D.*

Work without shaping to length E ending w s row.

Shape shoulder

Keeping patt constant, cast off 9(9, 10, 10, 11, 11) sts at beg next and foll 2 alt rows. Work 1 w s row. Cast off rem 8(10, 9, 11, 10, 12) sts.

2nd side

With r s of front facing, slip 25(27, 29, 31, 33, 35) sts at centre to a holder.

Rejoin yarn at right of rem sts and complete to match 1st side, reversing shaping by working neck edge decs as 'sl 1, K1, psso' on r s rows, and 'P2tog tbl' on w s rows, and by beg shoulder shaping on w s row.

SLEEVES

Using sm needles, cast on 51(51, 57, 57, 63, 63) sts – *measurement M, less allowance to tighten rib.*

Work in K1, P2 rib to length F ending r s row.

next row: rib as set inc 1 st at each end. 53(53, 59, 59, 65, 65) sts.

Change to lge needles and work in Broken rib patt, inc 1 st at each end

MEASUREMENTS REFER TO MOHAIR COWL DIAGRAM *(measurements in inches)*						
to fit chest	32	34	36	38	40	42
actual measurement (= twice A)	36	38	40	42	44	46
chest width (A)	18	19	20	21	22	23
centre back neck to cuff (B)	25½	26½	27½	28½	29½	30½
back neck width (C)	6	6½	7	7	7½	8
each shoulder width (D)	6	6¼	6½	7	7¼	7½
length to shoulder (E)	24½	25	25½	26	26½	27
welt and cuff depth (F)	3½	3½	3½	3½	3½	3½
body length to underarm (G)	15	15½	15½	16	16	16½
armhole depth (H)	9½	9½	10	10	10½	10½
shoulder shaping depth (J)	1	1	1	1	1	1
front neck shaping depth (K)	2	2	2	2	2	2
sleeve seam length (L)	16½	17	17½	18	18½	19
sleeve width at cuff (M)	8½	8½	9½	9½	10½	10½
sleeve width at top (N)	18	18	19	19	20	20

Note: centre back neck to cuff measurement (B) = ½ chest width (A) + sleeve seam length (L). Length to shoulder (E) = body length to underarm (G) + armhole depth (H).

MATERIALS

Avocet Tweed – gms (standard DK/worsted)	650	650	700	700	750	750

Needles for main parts (lge): 4mm (UK 8, US 5–6)

Needles for edgings (sm): 3¼mm (UK 10, US 3)

Set of 4 double-ended (dp) or circular sm needle(s) for neckband

3rd and foll 4th row, keeping patt constant over incs, until there are 107(107, 113, 113, 119, 119) sts – *measurement N*.
Work without shaping to length L ending w s row.
Cast off loosely in rib as set.

NECKBAND

Join shoulder seams. Using set of dp or circ sm needles, K up 37(39, 41, 43, 45, 47) sts from back neck; pick up and K 19(18, 18, 19, 18, 18) sts from left neck shaping; K up 25(27, 29, 31, 33, 35) sts from centre front and pick up and K 18(18, 17, 18, 18, 17) sts from right neck shaping.
99(102, 105, 111, 114, 117) sts.
round 1: *K1, P2 rep from * to end.
Repeat this round to length F ending at same point as start.
Cast off loosely in rib as set (use a larger needle for a looser edge).

TO MAKE UP

Join top edges of sleeves to armhole edges between marking threads. Join side and sleeve seams.
Fold neckband in half to inside and sew down neatly ensuring an easy fit over head.
If required, press lightly according to instructions on ball bands; but this rib stitch is usually best left without pressing.

FLOPPY SHIRT

TENSION/GAUGE

20 sts and 27 rows = 4″ measured over Seed stitch below using lge needles.

STITCHES USED

K1 P2 rib – multiple of 3 st:
   r s rows: K1, *K1, P2 rep from * to last 2 sts, K2.
   w s rows: K1, *P1, K2 rep from * to last 2 sts, P1, K1.
Seed stitch – multiple of 4 sts, plus 3:
   row 1: *K3, P1 rep from * to last 3 sts, K3.
   row 2: K1, *P1, K3 rep from * to last 2 sts, P1, K1.
St st.

BACK

Using sm needles cast on 90(93,

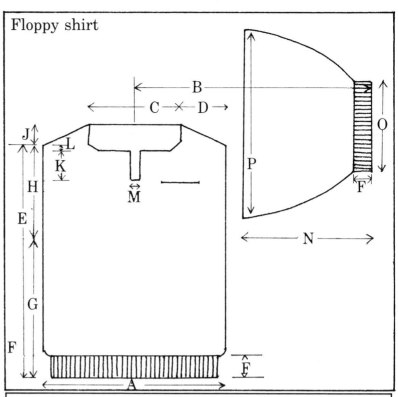

Floppy shirt

MEASUREMENTS REFER TO DIAGRAM (*measurements in inches*)

	30	32	34	36	38	40
to fit bust	30	32	34	36	38	40
actual measurement (twice A)	36	38	40	41½	43	44½
chest width (A)	18	19	20	20¾	21½	22¼
centre back neck to cuff measurement (B)	25	25½	26½	26¾	27¾	28¼
back neck width (C)	9	9½	10	10¼	10½	11
each shoulder width (D)	4½	4¾	5	5¼	5½	5¾
length to shoulder (E)	25¼	25¾	26½	26¾	27½	28
welt and cuff depth (F)	2½	2½	2½	2½	2½	2½
body length to underarm (G)	16½	17	17	17½	17½	18
armhole depth (H)	9¼	9¼	9½	9½	10	10
shoulder shaping depth (J)	1	1	1	1	1	1
front opening depth (K)	4	4	4	4	4	4
front neck shaping depth (L)	2	2	2	2	2	2
front opening width (M)	1	1	1	1	1	1
underarm sleeve length (N)	16	16	16½	16½	17	17
sleeve width at cuff (O)	12	12	12	12½	12½	12½
sleeve width at top (P)	18½	18½	19	19	20	20

Note: centre back neck to cuff measurement (B) = ½ chest width (A) + underarm sleeve length (N). Length to shoulder (E) = body length to underarm (G) + armhole depth (H).

MATERIALS

Rowan DK/worsted weight cotton

– gms	800	850	850	900	900	950

   Note: this is a DK/worsted weight cotton yarn, recommended st st tension gauge 19½ sts and 27 rows = 4″.

2 small buttons

Needles for main parts (lge): 4½mm (UK 7, US 7)

Needles for ribbing (sm): 3¾mm (UK 9, US 5)

96, 99, 105, 108) sts – *measurement A less allowance to tighten rib slightly.*
Work in K1 P2 rib to length F ending w s row. Change to lge needles.
next row: K, inc 1(2, 3, 4, 2, 3) sts evenly. 91(95, 99, 103, 107, 111) sts – *measurement A.* foll row: K1, P to last st, K1.
Work in Seed stitch to length G ending w s row.
Mark each end next row with a contrast thread. **
Work to length E ending w s row.

Shape shoulders

Keeping patt constant, cast off 8(8, 8, 9, 9, 9) sts at beg next 4 rows.
Cast off 7(8, 9, 8, 9, 10) sts at beg foll 2 rows.
Slip rem 45(47, 49, 51, 53, 55) sts – *measurement C* – on to a holder.

POCKET LINING

Using lge needles cast on 23 sts. Work in st st for 30 rows. Slip sts to a holder.

FRONT

Work as back to **.
Work to length E minus K and L, ending w s row.

Place pocket

next row: work 10(11, 12, 13, 14, 15) sts, slip next 23 sts to a holder and complete the row.
foll row: work to cast off sts, with P side of pocket lining facing, P across 23 sts; complete the row.

Divide for neck 1st side

next row: work 43(45, 47, 49, 51, 53) sts, turn. Leave rem 48(50, 52, 54, 56, 58) sts on a holder.
Work to length K ending w s row.
Total length = E minus L.

Shape neck

next row: work 29(30, 31, 32, 33, 34) sts, turn. Leave rem 14(15, 16, 17, 18, 19) sts on a holder.
2nd row: P2tog, work to end.
3rd row: work to last 2 sts, K2tog.
Repeat 2nd and 3rd rows once more.
6th row: as w s row.
7th row: as 3rd row.
Repeat these 2 rows once more.

23(24, 25, 26, 27, 28) sts rem – *measurement D.*
Work to length E ending w s row.

Shape shoulder

Keeping patt constant, cast off 8(8, 8, 9, 9, 9) sts at beg next and alt row. Work 1 w s row.
Cast off rem 7(8, 9, 8, 9, 10) sts.

2nd side

With r s of front facing, rejoin yarn at right of rem sts.
Cast off 5 sts at centre front – *measurement M* – and complete to match 1st side reversing shaping by working neck edge decs as 'sl 1, K1, psso' on r s rows and 'P2tog tbl' on w s rows, and beg shoulder shaping on a w s row.

SLEEVES

Using sm needles cast on 60(60, 60, 63, 63, 63) sts – *measurement O* – and work in K1, P2 rib to length F ending w s row.
Change to lge needles.
next row: K, inc 3(3, 3, 4, 4, 4) sts evenly. 63(63, 63, 67, 67, 67) sts.
foll row: K1, P to last st, K1.
Work in Seed stitch inc 1 st at each end 3rd and every foll 6th row until there are 91(91, 95, 95, 99, 99) sts – *measurement P* – keeping stitch patt constant over incs.
Work without shaping to length N ending w s row.
Cast off loosely.

NECKBAND

Join shoulder seams.
With r s of work facing, using sm needles, K up 14(15, 16, 17, 18, 19) sts from 2nd side of neck; pick up and K 15(14, 14, 15, 14, 14) sts from 2nd neck shaping; K up 45(47, 49, 51, 53, 55) sts from back neck; pick up and K 14(14, 13, 14, 14, 13) sts from 1st neck shaping, and K up 14(15, 16, 17, 18, 19) sts from 1st side of neck. 102(105, 108, 114, 117, 120) sts.
Work 5 rows K1, P2 rib beg and ending w s row.
Cast off in rib as set.

BUTTONHOLE BAND

With r s of front facing, using sm needles pick up and K 30 sts evenly from right side of front neck opening and side edge of neckband.

Work w s row of K1 P2 rib.
buttonhole row: rib 14 sts as set, P2tog, yrn/yo, rib 10, P2tog, yrn/yo, rib 2.
Work 3 more K1 P2 rib rows beg and ending w s row.
Cast off in rib as set.

BUTTON BAND

Work to match buttonhole band omitting button-holes. (5 rib rows in all, beg and ending w s row.)

TO MAKE UP

Join top edges of sleeves to armhole edges between marking threads. Join side and sleeve seams. Sew down pocket lining. Sew bands to centre cast off sts of front. Sew on buttons to match buttonholes.

POCKET TRIM

With r s of front facing, using sm needles, K across 23 sts on holder.
1st row: *K2 P1 rep from * to last 2 sts, K2.
2nd row: *P2 K1 rep from * to last 2 sts, P2.
Repeat these 2 rows once more.
5th row: as 1st.
Cast off in rib as set. Sew down side edges of pocket trim. Press according to instructions on ball bands.

SWIRLING LEAVES

(Measurements and materials, overleaf.)

TENSION/GAUGE

16 sts and 21 rows = 4″ measured over st st using lge needles and double yarn.

STITCHES USED

K1 P1 rib, st st.

BACK

Using sm needles and col A cast on 70(78, 86) sts and work in K1 P1 rib to measurement L, ending r s row.
Inc row: rib, inc 6 sts evenly across row. 76(84, 92) sts – *measurement A.*
Change to lge needles. Work in st

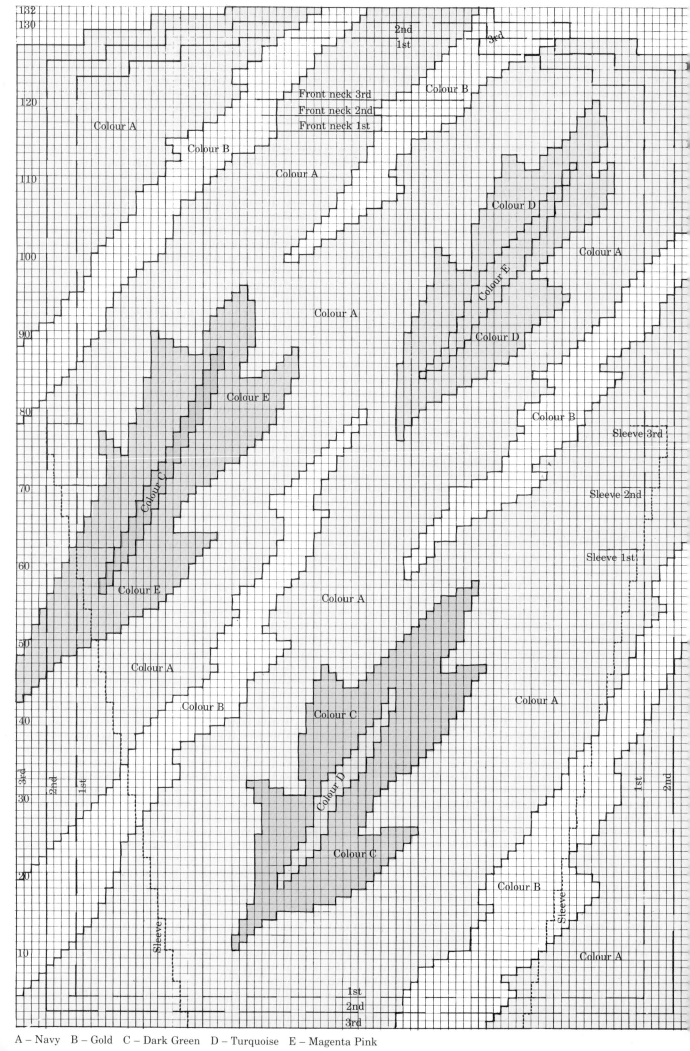

A – Navy   B – Gold   C – Dark Green   D – Turquoise   E – Magenta Pink

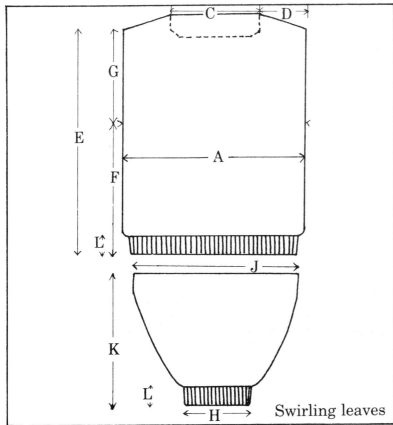

Swirling leaves

MEASUREMENTS REFER TO DIAGRAM *(measurements in inches)*

	30–32	34–36	38–40
to fit bust	30–32	34–36	38–40
actual measurement	38	42	46
chest width (A)	19	21	23
centre back neck to cuff (B) not shown on diagram = ½A + K	24½	26½	28½
neck width (C)	8	8½	9
shoulder width (D)	5½	6¼	7
length to shoulder (E)	25	26	27
length to armhole (F)	15½	16	16½
armhole depth (G)	9½	10	10½
cuff width (H)	8	8	8
top of sleeve width (J)	18½	19½	21½
sleeve length (K)	14½	16	17
welt and cuff depth (L)	2½	2½	2½

MATERIALS

Patons Diploma DK (standard DK/worsted wool USED DOUBLE THROUGHOUT)

col A Navy – gms	550	550	600
col B Gold – gms	150	150	150
col C Dark green – gms	150	150	150
col D Turquoise – gms	150	150	150
col E Magenta pink – gms	150	150	150

Needles for main parts (lge): 5½mm (UK 5, US 9)

Needles for ribbing (sm): 4½mm (UK 7, US 7)

Set of 4 double-ended (dp) or circular sm needles

st reading from chart beg chart row 5(3, 1) within outline of chosen size. Use a separate small ball for each area of col (see Intarsia knitting). Read r s rows right to left and w s rows left to right.

Mark each end chart row 73 with a contrast thread at *measurement F★.* Work to chart row 122(124, 126) (w s row – *measurement E.*)

Shape shoulders

Cast off 7(8, 9) sts at beg next 4 rows and 8(9, 10) sts at beg foll 2 rows.

Slip rem 32(34, 36) sts – *measurement C* – on a holder.

FRONT

Work as back to ★.

Work to chart row 116(118, 120) – *measurement E minus 1½"* – (w s row).

Shape neck 1st side

next row: work 26(29, 32) sts, turn.

Work on these sts only in cols as chart, dec 1 st at neck edge on foll 4 rows. 22(25, 28) sts rem – *measurement D.* Work 1 w s row – chart row 122(124, 126).

Shape shoulder

Cast off 7(8, 9) sts at beg next and alt row.

Work 1 w s row. Cast off rem 8(9, 10) sts.

2nd side

With r s of front facing, slip 24(26, 28) sts at centre to a holder and complete to match left side, working from chart, reversing shapings.

SLEEVES

Using sm needles and col A cast on 34 sts – *measurement H* – and work in K1 P1 rib to measurement L, ending r s row.

Inc row: rib, inc 10 sts evenly across row. 44 sts.

Change to lge needles and work in st st reading from chart within sleeve outline shown, inc 1 st at each end 3rd and every foll 4th row until there are 74(78, 82) sts – *measurement J.*

Work to chart row 62(70, 78) (w s row).

Total length = measurement K. Cast off loosely.

COLLAR

Join shoulder seams. With r s facing using dp or circ sm needles and col A, K up 32(34, 36) sts from back neck, pick up and K 10 sts from left neck shaping, K up 24(26, 28) sts from centre front, pick up and K 10 sts from right neck shaping. 76(80. 84) sts.

Work in rounds of K1 P1 rib for 9″, ending same point as start. Change to lge needle and cast off in rib.

TO MAKE UP

Join top edges of sleeves to armhole edges between markers. Join side and sleeve seams. Press according to instructions on ball bands.

CABLE MOTIF

TENSION/GAUGE

14 sts and 20 rows = 4″ over Caterpillar stitch below using lge needles.

STITCHES USED

K2 P2 rib – multiple of 4 sts:
 row 1: K1, *K2, P2 rep from * to last 3 sts, K3.
 row 2: K1, *P2, K2 rep from * to last 3 sts, P2, K1.
g st – all rows K.
Caterpillar stitch – multiple of 8 sts, plus 3.
 row 1: *K3, P5 rep from * to last 3 sts, K3.
 row 2 and every alt row: P.
 row 3: K.
 row 5: P4, *K3, P5 rep from * to last 7 sts, K3, P4.
 row 7: K.
 (row 8 as row 2)
Cable panel: 16 sts (= 2½″ width)
 row 1: P2, K12, P2.
 row 2: K2, P12, K2.
 rows 3–8: rep rows 1 and 2, 3 more times.
 row 9: P2, slip 6 sts to cable needle at back of work, K next 6 sts, K 6 from cable needle, P2.
 row 10: as row 2.
 rows 11–16: rep rows 1 and 2, 3 more times.

MAIN PIECE

Begin at lower front edge. Using sm needles cast on 64(72) sts – (*measurement A at main tension*) –

and work in K2 P2 rib to length F, ending row 1.
inc row: P4(6), *m 1, P8(4) rep from * to last 4(6) sts, m 1, P to end. 72(88) sts.
Change to lge needles.
row 1: K1, work 27(35) sts of row 1 of caterpillar stitch, 16 sts of row 1 of cable panel, 27(35) sts of caterpillar stitch, K1.

row 2: K1, work 27(35) sts of row 2 of caterpillar stitch, 16 sts of row 2 of cable panel, 27(35) sts of caterpillar stitch, K1.
Continue in this way working successive patt rows for 6 more rows, thus ending row 8 of patterns.
Note: Caterpillar stitch repeats over 8 rows and cable panel over 16 rows.

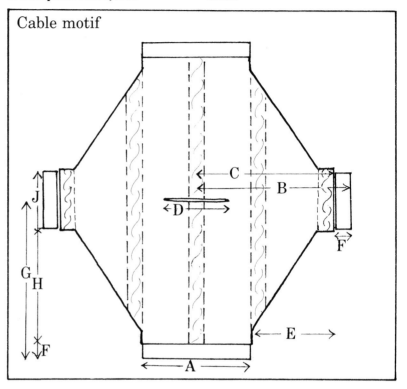

Cable motif

MEASUREMENTS REFER TO DIAGRAM (*measurements in inches*)

to fit bust	32–34	36–38
to fit hips	34–36	38–40
width across hips (A)	18	20
centre back neck to folded cuff (B)	24	28
centre back neck to top of cuff (C)	22	26
neck opening width (D)	12	12
sleeve extension (E)	16	18
cuff (to be folded) and welt depth (F)	4	4
length to shoulder (G)	26	29
body length to cuff level (H)	16	19
sleeve width at cuff (J)	12	12

Note: length to shoulder (G) = welt depth (F) + body length to cuff level (H) + ½ sleeve width at cuff (J).

MATERIALS

Yves Saint-Laurent Narvik (chunky/bulky tweed) – gms	800	850

Needles (long length) for main parts (lge): 5½mm (UK 5, US 9)

Needles for ribbing (sm): 4½mm (UK 7, US 7)

Circ needle for collar: 5mm (UK 6, US 8)

Cable needle.

Shape sleeves

Keeping pattern constant:
Inc 1 st at each end next and every alt row 16 times, working extra sts in st st and 1 st at each edge always in g st. 104(120) sts ending cable panel row 8.
Inc 1 st at each end next and every alt row 13(21) times, working st sts as cable panel to correspond with centre cable, with extra sts in caterpillar st and 1 st at each edge always in g st. 130(162) sts ending w s row.
Cast on 2 sts at beg next 14 rows keeping extra sts in caterpillar st with 1 st at each edge in g st. 158(190) sts ending cable panel row 16.
Next row: cast on 16 sts and work them as K1, P2, K12, P1; P next st; * work 27(35) sts caterpillar st; 16 sts as cable panel*, repeat * to * twice more, work 27(35) sts as caterpillar st, K1.
Foll row: cast on 16 sts and work them as K3, P12, K1; K next st; * work 27(35) sts caterpillar st; 16 sts as cable panel *, repeat * to * to last st, K1.
Cont in this way with 5 cable panels and 4 sets of caterpillar st and 1 st at each edge always in g st for a further 30 rows, thus ending cable panel row 16. 112(128) pattern rows.
190(222) sts – *twice width C and length G.*

Neck opening

Keeping patterns constant:
next row: pattern 71(87) sts, cast off next 48 sts, pattern 71(87) sts to end.
foll row: work in pattern casting on 48 sts across neck opening.

BACK

Work 30 rows in patt ending cable row 16.

Shape sleeves

Keeping pattern constant:
Cast off 16 sts at beg next 2 rows.
Cast off 2 sts at beg next 14 rows.
Dec 1 st at each end next and every alt row 29(37) times until 72(88) sts rem.
Work a further 7(9) patt rows, thus ending cable panel row 16.
Change to sm needles.
next row: K 4(6), *K2tog, K7(3) repeat from * to last 5(7) sts, K2tog, K to end. 64(72) sts.

Work in K2 P2 rib beg and ending row 2 to length F. Change to a lge needle. Cast off loosely in rib.
Back should match Front exactly.

CUFFS

With r s of work facing using sm needles, pick up and K 32 sts evenly from sleeve edge. Work in K2 P2 rib beg and ending row 2 to length F.
Change to a lge needle. Cast off in rib.

COLLAR

With r s of work facing, using circ needle for collar, pick up and K 48 sts from each edge of neck opening. 96 sts.
Work in rounds of K2 P2 rib (all rounds: *K2 P2 repeat * to end) to length 9" or as required.
Change to a lge needle and cast off in rib.

TO MAKE UP

Join side and underarm seams reversing seam on each cuff to allow for folding back.
Press according to instructions on ball bands.

SNOW WHITE

(Measurements and materials, overleaf.)

TENSION/GAUGE

26 sts and 26 rows = 4" over twist rib using lge needles; 24 sts and 30 rows using sm needles, slightly stretched.
21½ sts and 26 rows = 4" over diamond stitch using lge needles.

STITCHES USED

twist rib – multiple of 4 sts:
  row 1: K1, *twist 2 (= K 2nd st in front of 1st, K 1st st, slip both sts off needle), P2 rep from * to last 3 sts, twist 2, K1.
  row 2: K1, *P2, K2 rep from * to last 3 sts, P2, K1.
diamond pattern – multiple of 16 sts as chart.

BACK

Using sm needles cast on 104(112, 120) sts – *measurement A at rib tension on sm needles.*
Work in twist rib for 4" (*measure-*

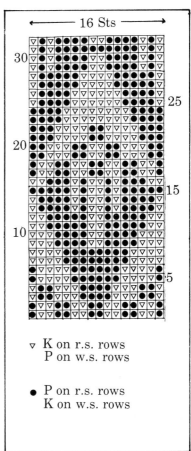

16 Sts

▽ K on r.s. rows
  P on w.s. rows

● P on r.s. rows
  K on w.s. rows

ment H) ending w s row, inc 1 st at each end last row. 106(114, 122) sts.
Change to lge needles.
next row: twist rib as set 37(41, 45) sts; work row 1 of diamond st chart, twice, reading left to right; twist rib as set 37(41, 45) sts.
foll row: twist rib as set 37(41, 45) sts; work row 2 of diamond st chart, twice, reading right to left; twist rib as set 37(41, 45) sts.

Shape sleeves

Keeping patterns as set, reading successive chart rows, inc 1 st at each end next and every alt row (with extra sts in twist rib) for 108(104, 100) rows until there are 214(218, 222) sts ending w s row on chart row 14(10, 6).
1st size only: cast on 6 sts at beg next 2 rows.
2nd size only: cast on 6 sts at beg next 4 rows and 8 sts at beg foll 2 rows.
3rd size only: cast on 6 sts at beg next 6 rows and 8 sts at beg foll 4 rows.
All sizes: 112 rows from top of welt – *measurement J* – 226(258, 290) sts – *twice measurement B at diamond stitch tension,* ending chart row 16.

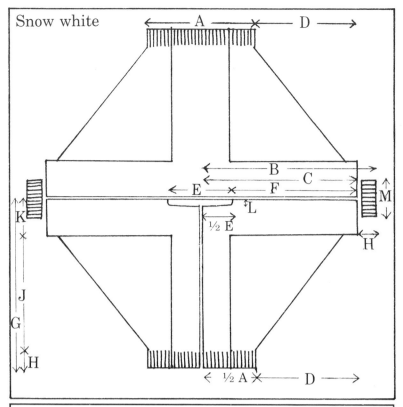

Snow white

Next row: K1, work row 17 of diamond st chart 14(16, 18) times, K1.

Foll row: K1, work row 18 of diamond st chart 14(16, 18) times, K1.

Keeping pattern as set, work to chart row 32, then rows 1–32 again. *48 chart rows = measurement K.* Cast off loosely in K & P as set.

LEFT FRONT

Using sm needles cast on 52(56, 60) sts – *½ measurement A at rib tension on sm needles.*

Work in twist rib for 4″ (*measurement H*) ending w s row, inc 1 st at each end last row. 54(58, 62) sts. Change to lge needles.

Keeping pattern constant, **next row:** twist rib as set 37(41, 45) sts; work row 1 of diamond st chart; K1.

foll row: K1; work row 2 of diamond st chart; twist rib as set 37(41, 45) sts.

Shape sleeves

Keeping patterns as set, reading successive chart rows, inc 1 st at beg next and every alt row (with extra sts in twist rib) for 108(104, 100) rows until there are 108(110, 112) sts ending w s row on chart row 14(10, 6).

1st size only: cast on 6 sts at beg next row.

2nd size only: cast on 6 sts at beg next and alt row and 8 sts at beg foll alt row.

3rd size only: cast on 6 sts at beg next and foll 2 alt rows and 8 sts at beg foll 2 alt rows.

All sizes: work to end, work 1 w s row. 112 rows from top of welt – *measurement J.* 114(130, 146) sts – *measurement C at diamond stitch tension,* ending chart row 16.

Next row: K1, work row 17 of diamond st chart 7(8, 9) times, K1.

Foll row: K1, work row 18 of diamond st chart 7(8, 9) times, K1.

Keeping pattern as set, work to chart row 32, then rows 1–16 again. *32 chart rows = measurement K minus L.*

Shape neck

Next row: pattern 102(118, 134) sts, turn. Leave rem 12 sts on holder.

Foll row: P2tog, pattern to end.

Foll row: pattern to last 2 sts, K2tog.

MEASUREMENTS REFER TO DIAGRAM *(measurements in inches)*

to fit bust	30–32	34–36	38–40
to fit hips	32–34	36–38	40–42
width across at hips (A)	17	19	21
centre back neck to cuff (B) folded back	23	26	29
centre back neck to top of cuff (C)	21	24	27
width of sleeve increasing (D)	9	10¾	12½
back neck width	5	5	5
neckline to cuff width (F)	18½	21½	24½
length to shoulder (G)	28	28	28
welt and cuff depth (H)	4	4	4
depth of sleeve increasing (J)	17	17	17
½ sleeve width above cuff (K)	7½	7½	7½
front neck shaping depth (L)	2	2	2
cuff width (M)	8	8½	9

Note: ½ back neck width (E) + neckline to cuff width (F) = centre back neck to top of cuff (C). Welt depth (H) + depth of sleeve increasing (J) + ½ sleeve width above cuff (K) = length to shoulder (G).

MATERIALS

Phildar Wilky (approx aran/sport weight) –

gms	950	1000	1050

Needles for main part (lge): 4½mm (UK 7, US 7)

Needles for ribbing (sm): 3¾mm (UK 9, US 4)

Open ended zip length 27½″ (70 cms)

Repeat last 2 rows once more. 98(114, 130) sts rem – *measurement F*.
Work to chart row 32.
Cast off loosely in K and P as set.

RIGHT FRONT

Work to match left front reversing pattern as follows:
1st row after welt: K1, work row 1 of diamond st chart; twist rib as set 37(41, 45) sts.
Reverse all shapings (work neck edge decs as skpo on r s rows and P2tog tbl on w s rows).

CUFFS

Join shoulder seams right down to sleeve edges – use invisible seam or firm backstitch, matching patterns exactly, leaving 2 centre patterns on back for neck edge.
With r s facing using sm needles pick up and K 52(56, 60) sts from sleeve edge – *measurement M at rib tension on sm needles* and work in twist rib (beg row 1) for 4″ – *measurement G* – ending row 2. (Cuff is to be folded back.) Cast off in rib as set.

NECK EDGE

With r s facing using sm needles K up 12 sts from holder at right front neck; pick up and K 16 sts to shoulder seam, 32 sts from back neck and 16 sts from left front neck shaping; K up 12 sts from holder at left front neck edge. 96 sts.
Work in twist rib (beg and ending row 2) for 4″.
Cast off in rib as set.

TO MAKE UP

Join underarm and cuff seams. Set in zip (see page 19). Fold neckband in half to inside and sew down neatly.

SUNBURST

TENSION/GAUGE

28 sts and 32 rows = 4″ measured over bobble lace pattern using lge needles.
24 sts = 4″ measured over st st using lge needles.

Stitches used

Special abbs
MB = make bobble thus: in next

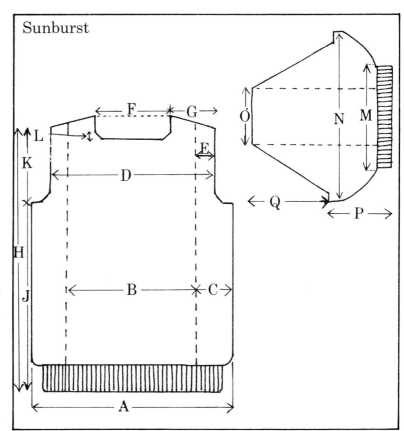

Sunburst

MEASUREMENTS REFER TO DIAGRAM (*measurements in inches*)

to fit bust	30	32	34	36	38	40
actual measurement (twice A)	33	35	37	39	41	43
width across bust (A)	16½	17½	18½	19½	20½	21½
pattern panel width (B)	12	12	12	12	12	12
side panel width (C)	2¼	2¾	3¼	3¾	4¼	4¾
width above armholes (D)	12½	13½	14	15	15½	16
side panel above armholes (E)	¼	¾	1	1½	1¾	2
neck opening width (F)	6	6	6¼	6¼	6½	6½
shoulder width (G)	3¼	3¾	4	4½	4½	5
length to shoulder (H)	19¼	20½	20½	21¾	21¾	23
length to underarm (J)	12½	13	13	13½	13½	14
armhole depth (K)	7¼	7½	7½	8¼	8¼	9
front neck depth (L)	1¼	1¼	1¼	1¼	1¼	1¼
sleeve width above elbow (M)	12½	12½	12½	13	13	13
sleeve width at underarm (N)	16½	16½	17	17	17½	17½
sleeve width at top edge (O)	4½	4½	4½	4½	4	4
sleeve length to underarm (P)	4¾	4¾	5½	5½	6	6
sleeve head depth (Q)	7¼	7¼	7¾	7¾	8½	8½

MATERIALS

Rowan lightweight DK worsted wool – gms Col 402	450	450	500	500	550	550

Needles for main part (lge): 3¾mm (UK 9, US 4)

Needles for ribbing (sm): 3mm (UK 11, US 2)

Set of double-ended (dp) or circular sm needles for neckband

st, K into back, front, back, front and back making 5 sts from 1; turn P5; turn, skpo, K3tog, slip 1st st over 2nd making 1 st.
K1b = knit st through back of loop.
K2 P2 rib – multiple of 4 sts:
  row 1: K1 *K2, P2 rep from * to last 3 sts, K3.
  row 2: K1 *P2, K2 rep from * to last 3 sts, P2, K1.
rev st st (reversed stocking stitch):
  r s rows: P
  w s rows: K.

Bobble lace pattern – multiple of 25 sts, plus 4:
  row 1: K1b *P2, K4, K2tog, K2, MB, K1, yrn/yo, K1b, P1, K1b, yrn/yo, K1, MB, K2, skpo, K4 rep from * to last 3 sts, P2, K1b.
  row 2 and every alt row: P1b, *K2, P10, P1b, K1, P1b, P10 rep from * to last 3 sts, K2, P1b.
  row 3: K1b, *P2, K1, MB, K1, K2tog, K4, yrn/yo, K1, K1b, P1, K1b, K1, yrn/yo, K4, skpo, K1, MB, K1 rep from * to last 3 sts, P2, K1b.
  row 5: K1b *P2, K2, K2tog, K2, MB, K1, yrn/yo, K2, K1b, P1, K1b, K2, yrn/yo, K1, MB, K2, skpo, K2 rep from * to last 3 sts, P2, K1b.
  row 7: K1b *P2, K1, K2tog, K4, yrn/yo, K3, K1b, P1, K1b, K3, yrn/yo, K4, skpo, K1 rep from * to last 3 sts, P2, K1b.
  row 9: K1b *P2, K2tog, K2, MB, K1, yrn/yo, K4, K1b, P1, K1b, K4, yrn/yo, K1, MB, K2, skpo rep from * to last 3 sts, P2, K1b.
  (row 10 as row 2)
  Rep these 10 rows.

BACK

Using sm needles cast on 96(100, 108, 112, 120, 124) sts – sts to give *measurement A at combination tension (see below) less allowance to tighten rib.*
Work in K2 P2 rib for 3″ ending r s row.
Inc row: rib 4(5, 6, 6, 8, 7) *m 1, rib 11(9, 12, 10, 13, 11)* repeat * to * to last 4(5, 6, 6, 8, 7) sts, m 1, rib to end.
105(111, 117, 123, 129, 135) sts – *79 centre sts at pattern tension for measurement B + sts at st st tension for measurement C each side.*
Change to lge needles.

next row: work 13(16, 19, 22, 25, 28) sts as row 1 of rev st st (*measurement C*), centre 79 sts as row 1 of bobble lace patt (*measurement B*), 13(16, 19, 22, 25, 28) sts as row 1 of rev st st (*measurement C*).
Continue with stitch patterns as set to length J ending w s row.

Shape armholes

**Keeping pattern constant:
Cast off 6 sts at beg next 2 rows.
dec row 1: P2tog, patt as set to last 2 sts, P2tog tbl.
foll row: work in patt. ******
Repeat these 2 rows 5(6, 7, 8, 9, 10) more times until 81(85, 89, 93, 97, 101) sts rem – *measurement D (= measurement B + twice measurement E).*
***Work to length H ending row 10.

Shape shoulders

Keeping patterns constant:
Cast off 4(4, 4, 5, 5, 5) sts at beg next 8 rows.
Cast off 3(5, 6, 4, 5, 7) sts at beg next 2 rows, thus ending row 10.
Slip rem 43(43, 45, 45, 47, 47) sts – *measurement F* – to a holder.

FRONT

Work as Back to *******.
Work to length H minus L – 10 rows less than Back.

Shape neck left side

next row: pattern 28(30, 32, 34, 36, 38) sts, turn.
Work on these sts only.
2nd row: cast off 5(5, 6, 6, 7, 7) sts, pattern to end.
3rd row: pattern to last 2 sts, K2tog.
4th row: work in pattern.
Repeat last 2 rows 3 more times. 19(21, 22, 24, 25, 27) sts rem – *measurement G* – ending row 10.

Shape shoulder

Keeping pattern constant:
Cast off 4(4, 4, 5, 5, 5) sts at beg next and foll 3 alt rows.
Work 1 w s row.
Cast off rem 3(5, 6, 4, 5, 7) sts.

Right side

With r s facing, slip centre 25 sts on a holder. Rejoin yarn and complete row on rem 28(30, 32, 34, 36, 38) sts.

Work 1 w s row. Complete to match Left side, reversing shaping by working neck edge decs as skpo on r s rows and beg shoulder shaping on a w s row.

SLEEVES

Using sm needles cast on 64(64, 64, 68, 68, 68) sts – *measurement M less allowance to tighten rib.* Work in K2 P2 rib for 1″ ending r s row.
inc row: rib 2 *m 1, rib 10(10, 10, 8, 8, 8)* repeat * to * to last 2 sts, m 1, rib 2.
75(75, 75, 77, 77, 77) sts – *measurement M with centre 29 sts at pattern tension + sts each side at st st tension.*
Change to lge needles.
next row: work 23(23, 23, 24, 24, 24) sts as row 1 of rev st st; centre 29 sts as row 1 of bobble lace patt; 23(23, 23, 24, 24, 24) sts as row 1 of rev st st.
Continue with stitch patterns as set, inc 1 st at each end every r s row (extra sts in rev st st) until there are 101(101, 105, 105, 109, 109) sts – *measurement N.*
Continue without shaping to length P ending row 10(10, 6, 6, 10, 10).

Shape sleeve head

Work as Back ****** to ******.
Repeat last 2 rows 28(28, 30, 30, 33, 33) more times until 31(31, 31, 31, 29, 29) sts rem – *measurement O* – ending patt row 10. *58(58, 62, 62, 68, 68) shaping rows = measurement Q.*
Cast off.

NECKBAND

Join shoulder seams.
With right side facing using dp or circ sm needles, K up 43(43, 45, 45, 47, 47) sts from back neck; pick up and K 16(16, 17, 17, 18, 18) sts from left neck shaping; K up 25 sts from centre front; pick up and K 16(16, 17, 17, 18, 18) sts from right neck shaping. 100(100, 104, 104, 108, 108) sts.
round 1: *K2 P2* repeat * to * to end.
Repeat this round till neckband measures 2″ ending complete round.
Cast off loosely in rib as set.

TO MAKE UP

Join side and sleeve seams. Set in sleeves, gathering top half of sleeve

shaping evenly to fit armhole.
Press lightly or block – do not
press ribbing; avoid over-pressing
stitch pattern.

FAIRISLE CARDIGAN

TENSION/GAUGE

36 sts and 38 rows = 4″ measured
over fairisle pattern using lge needles.

STITCHES USED

K2, P2 rib – multiple of 4 sts.
  row 1: K1, * K2, P2, rep from
  * to last 3 sts, K3.
  row 2: K1, * P2, K2, rep from
  * to last 3 sts, P2, K1.
fairisle pattern:
  as chart – multiple of 12 sts,
  plus 3. Strand yarns *loosely*
  across w s of work, twisting
  every 2 or 3 sts when passing
  behind 5 or more sts; always
  twist both cols at beg *every*
  row.

BACK

Using sm needles and col A cast on
152(164, 176, 188) sts and work in
K2 P2 rib to length F ending r s
row.
inc row: K1, * ml, rib 25(27, 29,
31) rep from * to last st, ml, K1.
159(171, 183, 195) sts – *measurement A at fairisle tension, adjusted to
multiple of 12 sts, plus 3.*
Change to lge needles.
row 1: K1A, * K12 sts of chart row
1 overleaf, reading right to left in
cols as shown; rep from * to last 2
sts, K st 1 of chart again, K1A.
row 2: K1A, P st 1 of chart row 2, *
P 12 sts of chart row 2 reading left
to right; rep from * to last st, K1A.
Cont in this way reading successive
chart rows until 120(120, 124, 124)
patt rows are complete thus ending
chart row 40(40, 4, 4) (w s row) –
length = measurement G.

Shape armholes

Cont in patt, shaping as follows:
Cast off 6 sts at beg next 2 rows.
dec row 1: skpo in A, patt to last 2
sts, K2tog in A.
dec row 2: work in patt.
Repeat these 2 rows, 11 more
times, until 123(135, 147, 159) sts
rem – *measurement B.*

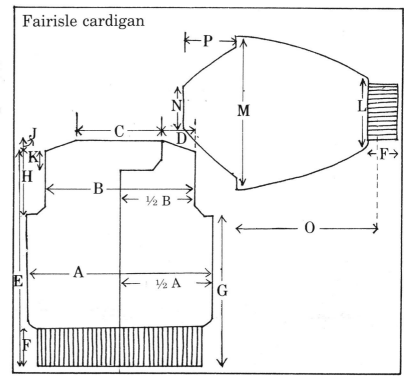

Fairisle cardigan

MEASUREMENTS REFER TO DIAGRAM (*measurements in inches*)

	32	34	36–38	40
to fit bust	32	34	36–38	40
actual measurement (twice A)	36	38	41	43
width across chest (A)	18	19	20½	21½
width across shoulders (B)	13½	15½	16½	17½
back neck width (C)	6	6½	7	7½
each shoulder width (D)	4	4½	4¾	5
length to shoulder (E)	25	25	26	26
welt and cuff depth (F)	4	4	4	4
body length to underarm (G)	16½	16½	17	17
armhole depth (H)	8½	8½	9	9
shoulder shaping depth (J)	1	1	1	1
front neck depth (K)	2	2	2	2
sleeve width above cuff (L)	10	10	11	11
sleeve width at armhole (M)	16	16	17½	17½
flat top of sleeve (N)	4	4	4	4
sleeve length with cuff folded back (O)	16½	16½	17	17
sleeve head depth (P)	5	5	5½	5½

Note: back neck width (C) + twice each shoulder width (D) = width
across shoulders (B). Body length to underarm (G) + armhole depth
(H) = length to shoulder (E). Width of each front = ½A.

MATERIALS

Pingouin Fil d'Ecosse no. 5 (3 ply/fingering weight cotton)

col A marine 03 (navy) – gms	400	450	450	450
col B celeste (pale blue) – gms	100	100	100	100
col C ecru 12 – gms	150	150	150	150
col D gris 31 (pale grey) – gms	100	100	100	100
col E buvard 33 (pale pink) – gms	100	100	100	100

Needles for main parts (lge): 3mm (UK 11, US 3)
Needles for ribbing (sm): 2¼mm (UK 13, US 1)
12 small buttons

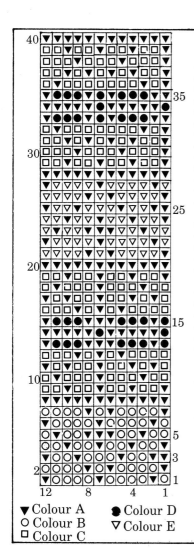

▼ Colour A   **●** Colour D
○ Colour B   **▽** Colour E
□ Colour C

Work without shaping until 80(80, 84, 84) patt rows are complete from beg of armhole shaping – *length H* thus ending chart row 40(40, 8, 8) (w s row).

Shape shoulders

Keeping patt constant, cast off 7(8, 9, 10) sts at beg next 10 rows.
1st & 2nd sizes only: work last 2 rows in col A.
Slip rem 53(55, 57, 59) sts – *measurement C* – to a holder.

LEFT FRONT

Using sm needles and col A cast on 76(84, 88, 96) sts and work in K2 P2 rib to length F ending r s row.
inc row: rib 2(2, 4, 4) sts, ★ m l, rib 18(40, 20, 44) sts, rep from ★ to last 2(2, 4, 4) sts, m l, rib to end. 81(87, 93, 99) sts – ½ *measurement A.*
Change to lge needles.
1st and 3rd sizes only: *multiple of 12 sts plus 9:* row 1: K1A, ★ K12 sts of chart row 1 reading right to left, rep from ★ to last 8 sts, K sts 1–7

again, K1A. *row 2:* K1A, P sts 7–1 of chart row 2 reading left to right, ★ P12 sts of chart row 2 reading left to right, rep from ★ to last st, K1A.
2nd and 4th sizes only: *multiple of 12 sts plus 3:* read chart rows as for back.
All sizes: Cont in this way reading successive chart rows until length matches back at beg armhole shaping thus ending chart row 40(40, 4, 4) (w s row).

Shape armhole

Keeping patt constant:
Cast off 6 sts at beg next row.
Work 1 w s row.
dec row 1: skpo in A, patt to end.
dec row 2: work in patt.
Rep these 2 rows, 11 more times, until 63(69, 75, 81) sts rem – ½ *measurement B.*
Work without shaping until 60(60, 64, 64) patt rows are complete from beg of armhole shaping thus ending chart row 20(20, 28, 28) (w s row). *Length = E minus K.*

Shape neck

next row: patt 43(48, 53, 58) sts, turn. Leave rem 20(21, 22, 23) sts on a holder.
2nd row: P2tog in A, patt to end.
3rd row: patt to last 2 sts, K2tog.
Repeat last 2 rows, 3 more times, until 35(40, 45, 50) sts rem.
Work without shaping until front matches back at shoulder edge thus ending chart row 40(40, 8, 8) (w s row).

Shape shoulder

Cast off 7(8, 9, 10) sts at beg next and foll 3 alt rows; work 1 w s row; cast off rem 7(8, 9, 10) sts (*1st & 2nd sizes only:* work last row in col A).

RIGHT FRONT

Work to match Left Front, reversing all shapings, but reverse patt as follows for **1st and 3rd sizes only:**
row 1: K1A, K sts 7–12 of chart row 1, ★ K12 sts of chart row 1 reading right to left, rep from ★ to last 2 sts, K st 1 again, K1A. *row 2:* K1A, P st 1 of chart row 2 ★ P12 sts of chart row 2 reading left to right, rep from ★ to last 7 sts, P sts 12–7 again, K1A. (2nd and 4th sizes, as left front.)

SLEEVES

Using sm needles and col A cast on 80(80, 88, 88) sts and work in K2 P2 rib to length F ending r s row.
inc row: Work in rib 4(4, 11, 11) sts, ★ m l, rib 4(4, 3, 3) sts, rep from ★ to last 4(4, 11, 11) sts, m l, rib to end. 99(99, 111, 111) sts – *measurement L.*
Change to lge needles and work in pattern as Back, beg row 21 inc 1 st at each end 3rd and every foll 6th row until there are 145(145, 157, 157) sts – *measurement M.*
Work without shaping until 140(140, 144, 144) patt rows are complete thus ending chart row 40(40, 4, 4).

Shape sleeve head

Keeping patt constant, cast off 6 sts at beg next 2 rows.
dec row 1: skpo in A, patt to last 2 sts, K2tog in A.
dec row 2: P2tog in A, patt to last 2 sts, P2tog tbl in A.
Rep these 2 rows until 45(45, 53, 53) sts rem ending dec row 2.
Cast off 4 sts at beg next 2(2, 4, 4) rows, thus ending chart row 8(8, 16, 16).
Cast off rem 37 sts – *measurement N.*

NECK EDGE

Join shoulder seams.
With r s of work facing, using sm needles and col A, K up 20(21, 22, 23) sts from left front neck holder; pick up and K 21 sts from left front neck shaping; K up 53(55, 57, 59) sts from back neck holder; pick up and K 22 sts from right front neck shaping and K up 20(21, 22, 23) sts from right front neck holder. 136(140, 144, 148) sts.
Beg rib row 2, work in K2 P2 rib for 1″ ending rib row 2.
Cast off in rib as set.

BUTTON BAND

Using sm needles and col A cast on 12 sts and work in K2 P2 rib to length matching left front edge, sewing band in position (slightly stretched) as work proceeds.
Ending w s row, cast off in rib as set.

BUTTONHOLE BAND

Mark positions for buttons on button band as follows: 1st at ½″ from lower edge, 12th at ½″ from top edge, rem 10 spaced evenly between.

Work to match button band making buttonholes as follows to match markers:

(r s row): work 5 sts in rib, cast off next 2 sts, rib to end.

foll (w s) row: rib, casting on 2 sts over buttonhole.

TO MAKE UP

Join side and sleeve seams. Set in sleeves.

Press according to instructions on ball bands.

Sew on buttons.

MAN'S FAIRISLE

TENSION/GAUGE

24 sts and 23 rows = 4″ measured over fairisle patt using lge needles.

STITCHES USED

K1 P2 rib – multiple of 3 sts, plus 2.

    r s rows: K1, *K1, P2 rep from * to last 2 sts, K2.

    w s rows: K1, *P1, K2 rep from * to last 2 sts, P1, K1.

Fairisle patt as chart worked in st st – multiple of 8 sts.

BACK

Using sm needles and col A cast on 110(116, 125, 131, 140) sts. Work in K1 P2 rib to length G ending w s row.

Inc row: rib as set inc 5(7, 6, 8, 7) sts evenly across row. 115(123, 131, 139, 147) sts – *measurement A at main tension.*

Change to lge needles.

row 1: K1A, *K 8 sts of chart row 1 in cols as shown overleaf, reading right to left rep from * to last 2 sts, K st 1 of chart again, K1A.

row 2: K1A, P st 1 of chart, *P 8 sts of chart row 2 reading left to right rep from * to last st, K1A.

Cont in patt as set working edge sts in appropriate col, breaking off and joining in cols at edge of work as required, until work measures length F ending w s row.

Shape armholes

Keeping patt constant, cast off 8 sts at beg next 2 rows. **

dec row 1: skpo in edge col, patt to last 2 sts, K2tog.

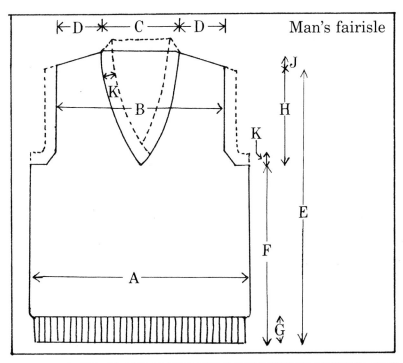

Man's fairisle

MEASUREMENTS REFER TO DIAGRAM (*measurements in inches*)

to fit chest	32	34–36	38	40	42–44
actual measurement (twice A)	38	41	44	46	49
width across chest (A)	19	20½	22	23	24½
width across shoulders excluding bands (B)	13¾	15	16½	17¾	19
back neck width (C)	5¾	6	6½	6¾	7
each shoulder width (D)	4	4½	5	5½	6
length to shoulder (E)	25	25½	26	26½	27
length to underarm (F)	16	16½	16½	17	17
welt depth (G)	2½	2½	2½	2½	2½
armhole depth (H)	9	9	9½	9½	10
shoulder shaping depth (J)	1	1	1	1	1
neck and armhole edge depth (K)	1	1	1	1	1

Note: width across shoulders (B) = back neck width (C) + twice shoulder width (D). Length to shoulder (E) = length to underarm (F) + armhole depth (H).

MATERIALS

Pingouin Type Shetland (standard DK/worsted yarn)

col A brown – gms	150	150	150	150	150
col B pale blue – gms	50	50	50	50	50
col C mid blue – gms	150	150	150	150	150
col D gold – gms	100	100	100	100	100
col E navy – gms	50	50	50	50	50
col F ecru – gms	100	100	100	100	100

Needles for main party (lge): 4mm (UK 8, US 5–6)

Needles for ribbing (sm): 3¼mm (UK 10, US 3)

Set of 4 double-ended (dp) or circular sm needles.

Safety pin; st holder

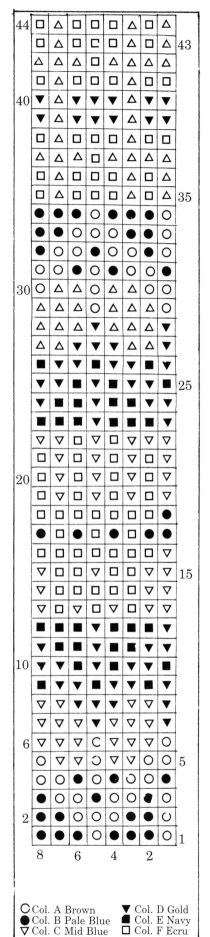

dec row 2: KI in edge col, patt to last st, KI in edge col.
Repeat these 2 rows until 83(91, 99, 107, 115) sts rem – *measurement B*.
Work without shaping to length E ending w s row.

Shape shoulders

Keeping patt constant cast off 8(9, 10, 11, 12) sts at beg next 6 rows.
Slip rem 35(37, 39, 41, 43) sts (*measurement C*) to a holder.

FRONT

Work as back to **.
99(107, 115, 123, 131) sts.

Shape neck left side

next row: skpo in edge col, patt 47(51, 55, 59, 63) sts, turn. Work on these sts only.
foll row: Work in patt.
Repeat dec rows 1 and 2 as for back until 34(38, 42, 46, 50) sts rem ending dec row 2.
Keeping armhole edge straight, cont dec at neck edge on every alt row until 26(29, 32, 35, 38) sts rem ending w s row.
*** Work 2 rows straight. Dec at neck edge on next row. Work w s row. *** Repeat *** to *** once more. 24(27, 30, 33, 36) sts rem – *measurement D*.
Work without shaping to length E, matching back at shoulder edge, ending w s row.

Shape shoulder

Cast off 8(9, 10, 11, 12) sts at beg next and alt row, work to end, work 1 w s row. Cast off rem 8(9, 10, 11, 12) sts.

Right side

With r s of front facing, slip 1 st at centre front to safety pin and rejoin cols at right of rem 49(53, 57, 61, 65) sts. Complete the row, dec 1 st (by K2tog) at end of row.
Complete to match left side reversing shaping (working neck edge decs as skpo and armhole edge decs as K2tog) and beg shoulder shaping on w s row.

NECK EDGE

Join shoulder seams.
With r s of work facing, using dp or circ needle sm size and col A,

begin at centre front: KI from pin; pick up and K 60(62, 63, 65, 65) sts from right front neck edge; K up 35(37, 39, 41, 43) sts from holder at back neck; pick up and K 60(62, 62, 64, 65) sts from left front neck edge. 156(162, 165, 171, 174) sts (*multiple of 3 sts*).
Work in rounds as follows:
round 1: KI, P2tog tbl, *KI, P2 rep from * to last 3 sts, KI, P2tog.
round 2: KI, P2tog tbl, *P2, KI rep from * to last 4 sts, P2, P2tog.
round 3: KI, P2tog tbl, PI, *KI, P2 rep from * to last 4 sts, KI, PI, P2tog.
Repeat these 3 rounds once more and round 1 again (7 rounds in all = 1").
Cast off in rib dec either side of centre front st as for round 2.

ARMHOLE EDGES

make 2
With r s of work facing, using sm needles and col A, pick up and K 110(110, 116, 116, 122) sts evenly from armhole edge (*multiple of 3 sts, plus 2*). Work in KI P2 rib beg and ending w s row for 7 rows.
Cast off in rib as set.

TO MAKE UP

Join side seams. Press according to instruction on ball bands.

SCOTTIE SWEATER

TENSION/GAUGE

23 sts and 28 rows = 4" measured over st st using lge needles.
23 sts = 4" measured over patt parts using lge needles: to achieve this tension, be sure *not* to pull yarns tightly.

STITCHES USED

KI PI rib.
st st – beg and end every P row with a K st.
Charts A and B: Strand yarns *loosely* across w s of work. Always twist both cols at beg *every* row.
Chart C: Use a ball of A for each side of motif rows 6–18. Strand A loosely across w s when working legs and tail.

BACK

Using sm needles and col A cast on 80(86, 92, 98, 104, 110) sts and work in K1 P1 rib to length F ending w s row, inc 1 st at end last row. 81(87, 93, 99, 105, 111) sts – *measurement A at st st tension adjusted to multiple of 6 sts, plus 3.* Change to lge needles.

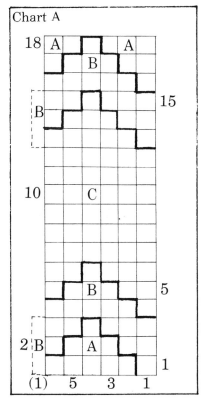

Chart A

Zig zag stripe

★★ next row: K1A, *K6 sts of chart A row 1 reading right to left in cols as shown rep from * to last 2 sts, K st 1 again, K1A.

foll row: K1A, P st 1 of chart A row 2, *P 6 sts of chart A row 2 reading left to right in cols as shown rep from * to last st, K1A. Cont in this way until chart A row 18 (P row) is complete. ★★ Change to col A. Work 2(4, 8, 12, 16, 20) rows st st ending P row.

First dog motif

next row: in A, K 38(44, 44, 50, 50, 56) sts; K 23 sts from chart B overleaf, row 1 reading right to left in cols as shown; in A, K rem 20(20, 26, 26, 32, 32) sts.
foll row: in A, K1, P 19(19, 25, 25, 31, 31) sts; P 23 sts from chart B row 2 reading left to right in cols as shown; in A, P 37(43, 43, 49, 49, 55) sts, K1.
Cont in this way until chart row 6

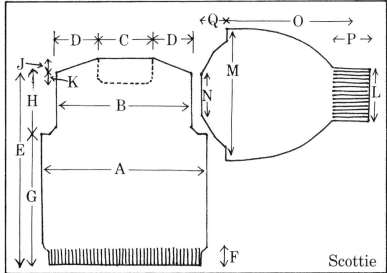

Scottie

MEASUREMENTS REFER TO DIAGRAM (*measurements in inches*)

to fit chest	24	26	28	30	32	34
actual measurement (twice A)	28	30	32	34	36	38
width across chest (A)	14	15	16	17	18	19
width across shoulders (B)	9	10	11	12	13	14
back neck width (C)	4½	5	5	5½	6	6½
each shoulder width (D)	2	2½	3	3¼	3½	3¾
length to shoulder (E)	15½	17	19	21	23	25
welt depth (F)	1½	2	2	2½	2½	3
body length to underarm (G)	10	11	12½	14½	16	17½
armhole depth (H)	6	6½	7	8	8½	9
shoulder shaping depth (J)	1	1	1	1	1	1
front neck depth (K)	2	2	2	2	2	2
cuff width (L)	6½	7	7¼	7½	8	8¼
sleeve width at armhole level (M)	11	12	13	14	15	16
flat top of sleeve (N)	3½	3¾	4	4½	4¾	5
sleeve length, cuff folded (O)	12	13½	15	16½	17	17½
cuff depth (P)	3	4	4	5	5	6
sleeve head depth (Q)	3	3	3½	3½	4	4

Note: back neck width (C) + twice each shoulder width (D) = width across shoulders (B). Body length to underarm (G) + armhole depth (H) = length to shoulder (E).

MATERIALS

Pingouin Confort (standard DK/worsted yarn)

col A navy 107 – gms	250	250	300	300	350	350
col B pale yellow 177 – gms	50	50	50	50	50	50
col C mid blue 170 – gms	100	100	100	150	150	150
col D pale pink 175 – gms	50	50	50	50	50	50
col E ecru 131 – gms	50	50	50	50	50	50

Needles for main part (lge): 4mm (UK 8, US 5–6)

Needles for ribbing (sm): 3¼mm (UK 10, US 3)

Set of 4 double-ended (dp) needles or circular sm needle.

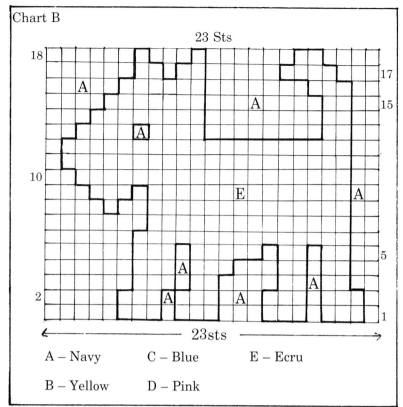

Chart B

23 Sts

18, 17, 15, 10, 5, 2, 1 (row markers)

←——— 23sts ———→

A – Navy   C – Blue   E – Ecru

B – Yellow   D – Pink

(P row) is complete.

next row: K1A, *K 6 sts from chart C row 1 reading right to left in cols as shown* rep * to * 5(6, 6, 7, 7, 8) more times, K st 1 again; K 23 sts from chart B row 7; rep * to * 3(3, 4, 4, 5, 5) times in all; K st 1 again, K1A.

foll row: K1A, P st 1 of chart C row 2, *P 6 sts of chart C row 2 reading left to right in cols as shown* rep * to * 2(2, 3, 3, 4, 4) more times; P 23 sts from chart B row 8; P st 1 of chart C row 2; rep * to * 6(7, 7, 8, 8, 9) times in all, K1A.

Cont in this way until 6 rows of chart C are complete.

Cont with chart B in position set with background in A until chart row 18 is complete (P row).

Change to col A. Work 2(4, 8, 12, 16, 20) rows st st ending P row.

Zig Zag stripe

Work ** to ** again.
Change to col A. Work 0(2, 6, 6, 10, 8) rows st st.

Shape armholes

Cast off 6 sts at beg next 2 rows.
Repeat next 2 rows 0(0, 0, 1, 1, 2) times:
dec row 1: skpo, work to last 2 sts, K2tog.
dec row 2: K1, work to last st, K1.

Second dog motif

next row: in A, skpo, K 14(20, 20, 25, 25, 30); K 23 sts from chart B row 1; in A, K 26(26, 32, 31, 37, 36) sts, K2tog.

foll row: in A, K1, P 26(26, 32, 31, 37, 36); P 23 sts from chart B row 2; in A, P 14(20, 20, 25, 25, 30), K1.

Cont with chart B in position set, dec each end chart rows 3 and 5, until chart row 6 (P row) is complete and 63(69, 75, 79, 85, 89) sts rem.

next row: in A, skpo, from chart C row 1, reading right to left, K sts 2–6(2–6, 2–6, 3–6, 3–6, 4–6), sts 1–6 1(2, 2, 3, 3, 4) times and st 1 again; K 23 sts from chart B row 7; K st 1 of chart C row 1, and sts 1–6 3(3, 4, 4, 5, 5) times and sts 1–5 (1–5, 1–5, 1–4, 1–4, 1–3) again, K2tog in A.

foll row: in A, K1; P 24(24, 30, 29,

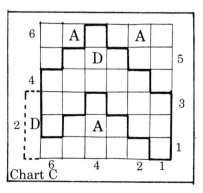

Chart C

6, 5, 4, 3, 2, 1 (row markers); 6, 4, 2, 1 (column markers)

35, 34) sts from chart C row 2 as set; P 23 sts from chart B row 8; P 12(18, 18, 23, 23, 28) sts from chart C row 2 as set; in A, K1.

Cont dec on every r s row as set until 51(57, 63, 69, 75, 81) sts rem – *measurement B* – at the same time completing chart C to row 6 and then chart B to row 18 (with background in A) working without shaping after dec is complete.

Change to col A, Work 2(4, 8, 12, 16, 20) rows st st ending P row.

Zig zag stripe

Work ** to ** again.
Change to col A. Work 2 rows st st.

Shape shoulders

Cast off 4(5, 5, 6, 7, 7) sts at beg next 4 rows and 4(4, 6, 6, 6, 8) sts at beg foll 2 rows.
Slip rem 27(29, 31, 33, 35, 37) sts – *measurement C* – to a holder.

FRONT

Work as Back to ***.
Work first 8 rows of Zig zag stripe ending 2 rows col C (*length E minus K*).

Shape neck

left side

Cont in Zig zag stripe beg. chart A row 9.

next row: K 18(20, 22, 24, 26, 28) sts, turn. Work on these sts only.

foll row: P2tog, work to end.

foll row: work to last 2 sts, K2tog.
Repeat last 2 rows twice more.
12(14, 16, 18, 20, 22) sts rem – *measurement D*.

Work until chart A row 18 (P row) is complete.

Change to col A. Work 2 rows st st.

Shape shoulders

Cast off 4(5, 5, 6, 7, 7) sts at beg next and alt row. Work to end.
Work 1 w s row.
Cast off rem 4(4, 6, 6, 6, 8) sts.

Right side

With r s of front facing, slip 15(17, 19, 21, 23, 25) sts at centre to holder and rejoin yarns at right of rem sts; complete the row and complete to match left side reversing shaping by working neck edge decs as skpo on r s rows and P2tog tbl on w s rows.

SLEEVES

Using sm needles and col A cast on 38(40, 42, 44, 46, 48) sts – *measurement L* – and work in K1 P1 rib to length P ending w s row and inc 1 st at end last row. 39(41, 43, 45, 47, 49) sts.
Change to lge needles and work in st st inc 1 st at each end next and every foll 4th row until there are 45(51, 51, 63, 63, 69) sts ending w s row.

Zig zag stripe

Work as back ** to **, inc on every 4th row as before, keeping patt constant over incs.
Change to col A and cont in st st inc as before until there are 63(69, 75, 81, 87, 93) sts.
Work without shaping to length O + ½P in all, (*to give length O with cuff folded*) ending w s row.

Shape top of sleeve

Cast off 6 sts at beg next 2 rows.
Rep dec rows 1 and 2 as for back until 31(35, 43, 47, 55, 59) sts rem.
dec row 3: as dec row 1.
dec row 4: P2tog, P to last 2 sts, P2tog tbl.
Rep these 2 rows until 21(23, 25, 27, 29, 31) sts rem. Cast off.

COLLAR

Join shoulder seams. Mark centre front st on holder. With r s of work facing using dp or circ sm needles and col A, K up 8(9, 10, 11, 12, 13) sts from centre front st to neck shaping; pick up and K 14 sts from right neck shaping; K up 27(29, 31, 33, 35, 37) sts from back neck; pick up and K 14 sts from left neck shaping; K up rem 7(8, 9, 10, 11, 12) sts from centre front. 70(74, 78, 82, 86, 90) sts.
Turn. Work in rows of K1 P1 rib inc 1 at at each end next and every alt row (work invisible inc 1 st in from each end) until there are 82(86, 90, 94, 98, 102) sts.
Work 1 row.

Shape collar

1st row: rib to last 4 sts, turn.
2nd row: sl 1, rib to last 4 sts, turn.
3rd & 4th rows: sl 1, rib to last 8 sts, turn.
Cont in this way for 6 more rows until 20 sts are unworked at each side.

11th & 12th rows: sl 1, rib to last 26 sts, turn.
13th row: sl 1, rib to end.
14th row: rib all sts.
Change to lge needle and cast off in rib.

TO MAKE UP

Join side and sleeve seams. Set in sleeves.
Press according to instructions on ball bands.
Swiss darn/duplicate stitch dogs' collars in col B as photo.

RAGLAN COAT

(Measurements and materials, overleaf.)

TENSION/GAUGE

15 sts and 18 rows = 4″ measured over st st on lge needles.

BACK

Using sm needles and col C cast on 76(80, 84, 88, 92, 96) sts – *measurement A at st st tension* – and work 7 rows g st. (*Odd no of rows makes neater lower edge.*)
Change to lge needles.

Block pattern

Work in Intarsia method.
* **row 1:** in col B, K 19(20, 21, 22, 23, 24); in col A, K 38(40, 42, 44, 46, 48); join in another ball of B and K 19(20, 21, 22, 23, 24).
row 2: K1, P each st in col as set to last st, K1.
Repeat these 2 rows 12(12, 13, 13, 14, 14) more times, 26(26, 28, 28, 30, 30) st st rows, ending P row.
** Change to col C. Work 8 rows g st.
Change to col D. Work 2 rows g st.
Change to col C. Work 8 rows g st.
***
next row: in col A, K 19(20, 21, 22, 23, 24); in col B K 38(40, 42, 44, 46, 48); in col A, K 19(20, 21, 22, 23, 24).
foll row: K1, P each st in col as set to last st, K1.
Repeat these last 2 rows 12(12, 13, 13, 14, 14) more times, ending P row.
Repeat g st rows ** to *** once.
Repeat once * to *** – *length = measurement E.*

Shape armholes

***** Work with cols in block patt beg at *** above, at the same time shaping as follows, keeping blocks constant over shaping:
Cast off 5 sts at beg next 2 rows.
dec row 1: sl 1, K1, psso, work to last 2 sts, K2tog.
dec row 2: K1, P each st in col as set to last st, K1. *****
Repeat these 2 rows until 30(38, 40, 48, 50, 56) sts rem ending w s row.
dec row 3: as dec row 1.
dec row 4: P2tog, P each st in col as set to last 2 sts, P2tog tbl.
Repeat dec rows 3 and 4 until 22(22, 24, 24, 26, 26) sts rem – *measurement C. Length = measurement E + F.* Cast off.

POCKET LININGS

make 2
Using lge needles and col A, cast on 20 sts and work in st st for 30(30, 32, 32, 34, 34) rows in all ending P row. Slip sts to a holder.

LEFT FRONT

Using sm needles and col C, cast on 38(40, 42, 44, 46, 48) sts – *measurement ½A at st st tension.* Work 7 rows g st.
Change to lge needles.

Block pattern

row 1: in col B, K 19(20, 21, 22, 23, 24); in col A, K 19(20, 21, 22, 23, 24).
row 2: K1, P each st in col as set to last st, K1.
Repeat these 2 rows 12(12, 13, 13, 14, 14) more times. 26(26, 28, 28, 30, 30) st st rows in all ending P row.
Work g st rows as back ** to ***.
**** **next row:** in col A, K 19(20, 21, 22, 23, 24) in col B, K 19(20, 21, 22, 23, 24).
foll row: K1, P each st in col as set to last st, K1.
Repeat these 2 rows 12(12, 13, 13, 14, 14) more times ending P row.
Change to col C. Work 8 rows g st.
Change to col D. K 1 row.

Place pocket linings

next row: K 9(10, 11, 12, 13, 14), cast off next 20 sts, K to end.
Change to col C.
next row: K 9(10, 11, 12, 13, 14) to cast off sts, with right side of pocket lining facing, K across 20 sts

121

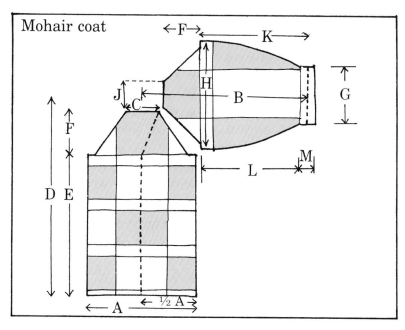

Mohair coat

MEASUREMENTS REFER TO DIAGRAM (*measurements in inches*)

to fit bust	30	32	34	36	38	40
actual measurement (= twice A)	40	42	44	46	48	50—
width across back (A)	20	21	22	23	24	25
width across each front (½A)	10	10½	11	11½	12	12½
centre back neck to folded cuff edge (B) with arm down	28	29	30	31	31¾	32½
back neck width (C)	6	6	6½	6½	7	7
finished length to shoulder (D)	36½	36½	38	38	39½	39½
body length to underarm (E)	25¾	25¾	26½	26½	27¼	27¼
raglan depth (F)	8¾	8¾	9½	9½	10¼	10¼
cuff width (G)	11½	12	12½	13	13½	14
sleeve width at armhole level (H)	18½	19½	20	21	21½	22½
flat top of sleeve (J)	4	4	4	4	4	4
finished underarm sleeve with cuff folded (K)	17	17½	17½	18	18	18½
sleeve length top of cuff to underarm (L)	15½	16	16	16½	16½	17
cuff depth (M)	3	3	3	3	3	3

Note: B = ½C + F + L + ½M. D = E + F + ½J.

MATERIALS

Phildar Falbadouce (standard mohair)

col A bleu france 11 – gms	360	400	400	400	440	440
col B suie 91 – gms	280	280	280	320	320	320
col C ondine 69 – gms	280	280	280	320	320	320
col D noir 67 – gms	80	80	80	80	80	80

6 large buttons

Needles for main parts (lge): 5½mm (UK 5, US 9)

Needles for edgings (sm): 4½mm (UK 7, US 7)

Stitch holders

from holder, K rem 9(10, 11, 12, 13, 14) sts to end.
Work 7 more rows g st.
Repeat first 26(26, 28, 28, 30, 30) rows again and g st rows ** to *** once more. *Length = measurement E.*

Shape armhole and neck

With cols in block pattern beg ****, keep pattern constant while shaping as follows: cast off 5 sts at beg next row. Foll row: patt as set. Dec 1 st at armhole edge (by skpo) on next and every right side row, AT THE SAME TIME dec 1 st at neck edge (by K2tog) on next and every foll 4th row, until 6(11, 11, 16, 17, 20) sts rem ending w s row. Dec 1 st at armhole edge (by skpo on r s rows and P2tog tbl, on w s rows) on every row and work 0(1, 2, 3, 3, 4) more decs as set at neck edge until 2 sts rem, ending w s row. Cast off. *Length = measurement E + F.*

RIGHT FRONT

Work to match left front reversing block patt and reversing shaping by working neck edge decs as 'sl 1, K1, psso' on K rows, and armhole edge decs as 'K2tog' on K rows and 'P2tog tbl' on P rows.

SLEEVES

Using sm needles and col C cast on 44(46, 48, 50, 52, 54) sts – *measurement G* – and work in g st to length M ending even no of rows.
Change to lge needles.

Block pattern

row 1: in col A, K8; in col B, K 28(30, 32, 34, 36, 38); join in another ball of A, K8.
row 2: K1, P each st in col as set to last st, K1.
Work with blocks in position as set, at the same time inc 1 st at each end next and every foll 4th row until there are 70(72, 74, 76, 78, 80) sts with 16 sts in col B at each side.
Work without shaping to length K ending P row.
Work g st rows ** to *** as for back once.

Shape sleeves

As for back ***** to *****.
Repeat dec rows 1 and 2 until 22(30, 30, 38, 38, 44) sts rem.

Repeat dec rows 3 and 4 until 14 sts rem ending w s row – *measurement J*. Cast off.

FRONT BANDS AND COLLAR

Join raglan seams matching blocks.

Using sm needles and col A cast on 12 sts. Work in g st working buttonholes as below at the foll lengths from cast on edge: 3½"(3½", 3¾", 3¾", 3¾", 4", 4"), and then ever foll approx 4¼" 5 more times to match up with stripes on front edge as follows when sewn together:
2nd, 4th & 6th buttonholes should match stripes in col D, with 3rd and 5th halfway between.
buttonhole row: K5, cast off next 2 sts, K to end.
foll row: K, casting on 2 sts over buttonhole.
Work without shaping until band measures as front edge to beg of neck shaping. Inc 1 st at each end of next and every foll 4th row until there are 29(29, 30, 30, 31, 31) sts. Work without shaping until piece equals front plus neck edge round to left front raglan seam. Dec 1 st at each end of next and every foll 4th row until 12 sts rem. Work without shaping until piece measures as front and neck edges all the way round. Cast off.

TO MAKE UP

Join side and sleeve seams. Sew down pocket linings. Sew bands and collar in position.
Press according to instructions on ball bands.
Sew on buttons to match buttonholes.
Brush with a teazle to raise pile on mohair if required.
With col D, embroider lines of chain st up lines of block pattern as illustrated.

CHRISTMAS

TENSION/GAUGE

14 sts and 20 rows = 4" measured over st st using lge needles.

STITCHES USED

st st.
K1 P1 rib.
g st (all rows K).

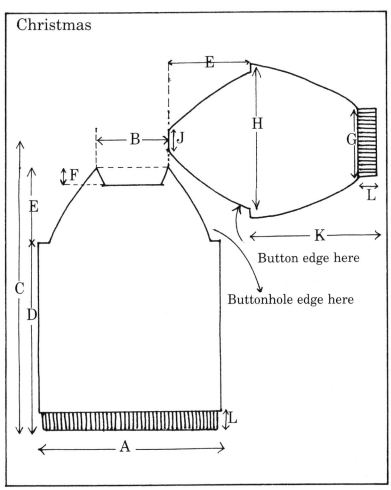

Christmas

Button edge here

Buttonhole edge here

MEASUREMENTS REFER TO DIAGRAM *(measurements in inches)*

to fit bust	30	32	34	36	38	40
actual measurement (twice measurement A)	36	38	40	42	44	46
width across at bust (A)	18	19	20	21	22	23
neck opening width (B)	8	8	8½	8½	9	9
length including ½ sleeve top (C)	26	26½	27	27½	28	28½
length to underarm (D)	17	17½	17½	17½	18	18½
depth, raglan shaping (E)	8	8	8	8½	8½	8½
depth, front neck shaping (F)	2	2	2	2	2	2
cuff width (G)	8	8	8½	8½	9	9
sleeve width at underarm (H)	16½	17	17½	18	18½	19
top edge of sleeve (J)	2	2	2½	2½	2½	2½
underarm sleeve length (K)	14	14½	15	15	15½	15½
welt and cuff depth (L)	2½	2½	2½	2½	2½	2½

MATERIALS

Pingouin Contrastes – gms	400	400	400	450	450	500

Needles for main part (lge): 5mm (UK 6, US 8)

Needles for ribbing (sm): 4mm (UK 8, US 5–6)

4 buttons

BACK

Using sm needles cast on 56(60, 64, 68, 72, 76) sts – *sts for measurement A at st st tension less allowance to tighten rib.*
Work in K1 P1 rib to length L ending r s row.
Inc 6 sts evenly across next row.
62(66, 70, 74, 78, 82) sts *to give measurement A at st st tension.*
Change to lge needles. Work in st st to length D ending w s row.

Shape raglan armholes

Cast off 4 sts (*approx 1"*) at beg next 2 rows. 54(58, 62, 66, 70, 74) sts rem.
1st, 2nd, 3rd, 4th and 5th sizes only:
dec row 1: K1, skpo, K to last 3 sts, K2tog, K1.
Work 3 rows without shaping.
Repeat these 4 rows 6(4, 3, 2, 1) more times, ending 4th row.
40(48, 54, 60, 66) sts rem.
28(20, 16, 12, 8) shaping rows complete.
All sizes: 40(48, 54, 60, 66, 74) sts rem.
next row: as dec row 1 above.
Work 1 row without shaping. **★★**
Repeat these 2 rows 5(9, 11, 14, 16, 20) more times ending 2nd row. 28(28, 30, 30, 32, 32) sts rem – *measurement B. 40(40, 40, 42, 42, 42) shaping rows complete in all = measurement E.*
Slip sts to a holder.

FRONT

Work as Back to **★★**
2nd, 3rd, 4th, 5th and 6th sizes only:
Repeat last 2 rows 4(6, 9, 11, 15) more times ending w s row.
All sizes: 38(38, 40, 40, 42, 42) sts rem.
30(30, 30, 32, 32, 32) shaping rows complete in all = measurement E minus F

Shape neck left side

1st row: K1, skpo, K8, turn.
Work on these sts only.
2nd row: P.
3rd row: K1, skpo, K to last 3 sts, K2tog, K1.
Repeat last 2 rows until 4 sts rem ending w s row.
9th row: K1, K3tog.
10th row: K2.
Cast off.

124

40(40, 40, 42, 42, 42) shaping rows complete in all to match Back.

Right side

With r s of front facing, slip centre 16(16, 18, 18, 20, 20) sts onto a holder, complete the row and complete to match left side reversing shaping by working neck edge decs as K1 skpo, and armhole edge decs as K2tog K1, all on r s rows.

SLEEVES

Using sm needles cast on 30(30, 32, 32, 34, 34) sts – *measurement G.*
Work in K1 P1 rib to length L, ending r s row.
Inc 4 sts evenly across next row.
34(34, 36, 36, 38, 38) sts.
Change to lge needles and work in st st inc 1 st at each end next and every foll 4th row until there are 58(60, 62, 64, 66, 68) sts – *measurement H.*
Work without shaping to length K ending w s row.

Shape raglan sleeves

Cast off 4 sts – *approx 1" to match Front/Back* – at beg next 2 rows.
50(52, 54, 56, 58, 60) sts rem.
dec row 1: as for Back.
Work 1 row without shaping.
Repeat these 2 rows 18(17, 16, 18, 17, 16) more times until 12(16, 20, 18, 22, 26) sts rem ending w s row.
38(36, 34, 38, 36, 34) shaping rows complete.
next row: as dec row 1.
foll row: K1, P2tog, P to last 3 sts, P2tog tbl, K1.
Repeat these 2 rows 0(1, 2, 1, 2, 3) more times until 8(8, 8, 10, 10, 10) sts rem ending w s row.
40(40, 40, 42, 42, 42) shaping rows complete in all = measurement E to match Back.
Slip sts to a holder.

NECKBAND

Join 3 raglan seams leaving right front raglan open. With right side facing, using sm needles, pick up and K 6 sts from left shaping, K up 16(16, 18, 18, 20, 20) sts from holder, pick up and K 6 sts from right shaping, K up 8(8, 8, 10, 10, 10) sts from right sleeve, 28(28, 30, 30, 32, 32) sts from back and 8(8, 8, 10, 10, 10) sts from left sleeve.
72(72, 76, 80, 84, 84) sts. Turn.
Work in g st for 2½" ending w s row.
Cast off using yarn double.

BUTTONHOLE EDGE

With r s of front facing, using lge needles, pick up and K 38(38, 38, 40, 40, 40) sts evenly from sloping raglan edge (not incl. cast off 1" step) and 12 sts from side edge of neckband. 50(50, 50, 52, 52, 52) sts.
Work 1 row g st.
buttonhole row: K 10(10, 10, 12, 12, 12) *cast off 2 sts, 1 st on r h needle, K next 9 sts* repeat ★ to ★ to last 4 sts. Cast off 2 sts. K to end.
follw row: K casting on 2 sts over each buttonhole.
Work 2 more rows g st.
Cast off using double yarn.

BUTTON EDGE

Work to match buttonhole edge omitting buttonholes (5 rows in all).

TO MAKE UP

Join cast off 1" step at left underarm. Join side and sleeve seams.
Sew on buttons to match buttonholes.
Press according to instructions on ball bands.

HIS AND HERS
TENSION/GAUGE

14 sts and 20 rows = 4" measured over st st using lge needles.

STITCHES USED

Special abbs
C6B – cable 6 sts thus: slip next 3 sts to cable needle, hold at back of work, K next 3 sts, then 3 sts from cable needle.
C6F – cable 6 sts as C6B but hold cable needle at front of work.
C5R – slip 2 sts to cable needle, hold at back of work, K next 3 sts and P2 sts from cable needle.
C5L – slip 3 sts to cable needle, hold at front of work, P next 2 sts and K 3 sts from cable needle.
MB – make bobble: in next st, K into front, back, front and back (4 sts from 1); turn; P4; sl 1, K3tog, psso. Push bobble to front of work on next row.

K1 P1 rib.
st st.
rev st st.

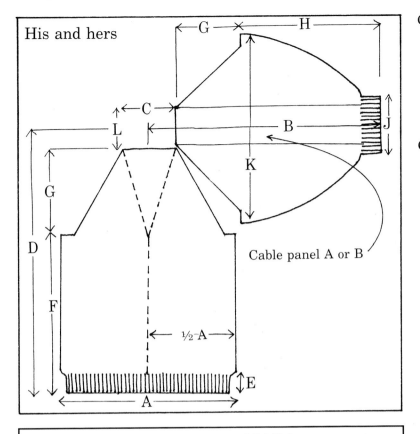

His and hers

Cable panel A or B

MEASUREMENTS REFER TO DIAGRAM (*measurements in inches*)

to fit bust/chest	32	34	36	38	40	42
actual measurement (= twice A)	36	38	40	42	44	46
chest width (A)	18	19	20	21	22	23
centre back neck to cuff (B)	27¾	28¾	29	30	30½	31½
back neck width (C)	5½	5½	5¾	5¾	6	6
finished length (D)	27	27½	28	28½	29	29½
welt and cuff length (E)	3	3	3	3	3	3
body length to underarm (F)	17½	17½	18	18	18½	18½
raglan depth (G)	8	8½	8½	9	9	9½
underarm sleeve length (H)	17	17½	17½	18	18½	19
sleeve width at cuff (J)	8¼	8¼	9	9	9½	9½
sleeve width at underarm (K)	15	15½	16¼	16¾	17½	18
sleeve head width at neck edge (L)	3	3	3	3	3	3

Note: finished length (D) = body length to underarm (F) + raglan depth (G) + ½ sleeve head width at neck edge (L). Centre back neck to cuff (B) = ½ back neck width (C) + raglan depth (G) + underarm sleeve length (H).

MATERIALS

Rowan Bright Tweed: (chunky/bulky)

Cardigan – gms + 6 medium buttons	850	850	850	900	900	950
Sweater – gms	800	800	800	850	850	850

Needles for main parts (lge): 6mm (UK 4, US 10)

Needles for ribbing (sm): 4½mm (UK 7, US 7)

Sweater only: set of 4 double-ended (dp) or circ sm needle(s): size, as above.

Cable panel A (width 13 sts):
  row 1: K6, P1, K6.
  row 2: P6, K1, P6.
  rows 3 and 4: as rows 1 and 2.
  row 5: C6B, P1, C6F.
  row 6: as row 2.
  rows 7 and 8: as rows 1 and 2.
  rows 9 and 10: as rows 1 and 2.
  Repeat these 10 rows.

Cable Panel B (width 13 sts):
  row 1: P3, MB, P5, K3, P1.
  row 2: K1, P3, K9.
  row 3: P7, C5R, P1.
  row 4: K3, P3, K7.
  row 5: P5, C5R, P3.
  row 6: K5, P3, K5.
  row 7: P3, C5R, P5.
  row 8: K7, P3, K3.
  row 9: P1, C5R, P7.
  row 10: K9, P3, K1.
  row 11: P1, K3, P5, MB, P3.
  row 12: as row 10.
  row 13: P1, C5L, P7.
  row 14: as row 8.
  row 15: P3, C5L, P5.
  row 16: as row 6.
  row 17: P5, C5L, P3.
  row 18: as row 4.
  row 19: P7, C5L, P1.
  row 20: as row 2.
  Repeat these 20 rows.

CARDIGAN BACK

Using sm needles cast on 60(64, 68, 72, 76, 80) sts.
Work in K1 P1 rib to length E ending w s row.
Change to lge needles and work in rev st st (beg with a P row) and inc 1 st at each end 1st row.
62(66, 70, 74, 78, 82) sts – *measurement A at st st tension.*
Work in rev st st to length F ending w s (K) row. **

Shape armholes

Cast off 4 sts at beg next 2 rows.
1st size only:
dec row 1: (r s row): K2, sl 1, K1, psso, P to last 4 sts, K2tog, K2.
dec row 2: K1, P2, K to last 3 sts, P2, K1.
dec row 3: K3, P to last 3 sts, K3.
dec row 4: as dec row 2.
Repeat these 4 rows once more. 50 sts rem. 8 shaping rows complete.
Repeat dec rows 1 and 2 only until 18 sts rem ending dec row 2.
2nd size only:
Work dec rows 1–4 as 1st size, once only. Repeat dec rows 1 and 2 until 18 sts rem ending dec row 2.
3rd size only:
Repeat dec rows 1 and 2 as 1st size until 20 sts rem ending dec row 2.

4th, 5th and 6th sizes only:
Repeat dec rows 1 and 2 as 1st size until 24(30, 34) sts rem ending dec row 2.
next row: as dec row 1.
foll row: K1, P1, P2tog, K to last 4 sts, P2tog tbl, P1, K1.
Repeat these 2 rows until 20(22, 22) sts rem.
All sizes:
40(42, 42, 44, 44, 46) shaping rows – *measurement G.* Slip rem 18(18, 20, 20, 22, 22) sts – *measurement C* – to a holder.

LEFT FRONT

Using sm needles cast on 30(32, 34, 36, 38, 40) sts and work in K1 P1 rib to length E ending w s row. Change to lge needles and work in rev st st inc 1 st at end 1st row. 31(33, 35, 37, 39, 41) sts – *½ measurement A.*
Work in rev st st to length F ending w s row.

Shape armhole and neck

Dec 1 st at neck edge at end of next and every foll 4th row by working last 2 sts as K2tog, 8(8, 9, 9, 10, 10) times in all, AT THE SAME TIME dec at armhole edge as follows:
cast off 4 sts at beg next row, work 1 row.
*** 1st size only:
dec row 1: (r s row): K2, sl 1, K1, psso, P to end (dec for neck as above if required).
dec row 2: K to last 3 sts, P2, K1.
dec row 3: K3, P to end.
dec row 4: as dec row 2.
Repeat these 4 rows once more. Repeat dec rows 1 and 2 only, working neck decs on every 4th row as set, until 8 neck decs are complete, then continue dec at armhole edge only as set until 2 sts rem. Cast off.
2nd size only:
Work dec rows 1–4 as 1st size, once only. Repeat dec rows 1 and 2 only working neck edge decs on every 4th row as set until 8 neck decs are complete, then cont dec at armhole edge only until 2 sts rem. Cast off.
3rd size only:
Repeat dec rows 1 and 2 as for 1st size, working neck edge decs on every 4th row as set, until 9 neck edge decs are complete, then cont dec at armhole edge only until 2 sts rem. Cast off.

4th, 5th and 6th sizes only:
Repeat dec rows 1 and 2 as for 1st size, working neck edge decs on every 4th row as set, until 9(10, 10) neck edge decs are complete, then cont dec at armhole edge only until 4(6, 6) sts rem, ending with dec row 2.
next row: as dec row 1.
foll row: 4th size only: P2tog, tbl, K1. Cast off rem 2 sts.
5th and 6th sizes only: K1, P2tog tbl, P1, K1.
next row: as dec row 1.
foll row: P2tog tbl, K1. Cast off rem 2 sts.
All sizes:
40(42, 42, 44, 44, 46) shaping rows – *measurement G.*

RIGHT FRONT

Work to match Left Front reversing all shaping by working armhole edge decs as 'K2tog, K2' on r s rows and neck edge decs as 'sl 1, K1, psso' on r s rows.

POCKETS

make 2
Using lge needles cast on 21 sts.
row 1: K1, P3, work 13 sts of row 1 of cable panel A, P3, K1.
row 2: K4, work 13 sts of row 2 of cable panel A, K4.
Cont in this way until 10 cable panel rows are complete. Repeat these 10 rows once more.
Change to sm needles. Dec 1 st at beg 1st row (20 sts), work 6 rows K1 P1 rib.
Cast off in rib as set.

SLEEVES

Using sm needles cast on 40(40, 42, 42, 44, 44) sts and work in K1 P1 rib to length E ending w s row and inc 1 st at end last row.
41(41, 43, 43, 45, 45) sts – *measurement J.*
Change to lge needles.
row 1: K1, P 13(13, 14, 14, 15, 15), work 13 sts of row 1 of cable panel A, P 13(13, 14, 14, 15, 15), K1.
row 2:
K 14(14, 15, 15, 16, 16), work 13 sts of row 2 of cable panel A, K 14(14, 15, 15, 16, 16).
Cont in this way, inc 1 st at each end next and every foll 8th row, repeating the 10 cable panel rows as required until there are 53(55, 57, 59, 61, 63) sts – *measurement K* – with extra sts in rev st st as set.

Work without shaping to length H ending w s row.

Shape raglan sleeve

Keep cable panel constant throughout.
Cast off 4 sts at beg next 2 rows.
Repeat dec rows 1–4 as 1st size of back until 35(37, 41, 43, 47, 49) sts rem ending dec row 4.
Repeat dec rows 1 and 2 as back until 15 sts rem – *measurement L* – ending dec row 2. Slip these sts to a holder.
All sizes: 40(42, 42, 44, 44, 46) shaping rows – *measurement G.*

BUTTONHOLE BAND

Join raglan seams taking in a seam of 1 st from each edge.
With r s of work facing, using sm needles, pick up and K the foll sts from Right Front edge for a ladies' cardigan and Left Front edge for a man's:
side edge of rib rows: 12 sts.
half back neck edge to centre: 8(8, 9, 9, 10, 10) sts, dec 1 st at back raglan seam; **from top of sleeve** 13 sts, dec 1 st at each seam; **rem front edge:** 75(77, 80, 82, 85, 87) sts.
108(110, 114, 116, 120, 122) sts.
Work 2 rows K1 P1 rib.
buttonhole row: K1 P1, K2tog, yrn/yo, [K1 P1] 3 times *K2tog, yrn/yo, work 8(8, 8, 10, 10, 10) sts in rib.* Repeat * to * 3 more times, K2tog, yrn/yo, rib to end.
Work 2 more rib rows, thus ending w s row.
Cast off in rib as set.

BUTTON BAND

Work to match buttonhole band omitting buttonholes (5 rib rows in all).

TO MAKE UP

Join bands at centre back neck. Join side and sleeve seams. Sew on pockets as illustrated.
Press according to instructions on ball bands.
Sew on buttons to match buttonholes.

V NECK PULLOVER

Instructions for the pullover below refer to cardigan instructions. The bodice and main parts of sleeves are worked in st st, but the decreases of the raglan shapings should be worked as for cardigan, for example:

r s dec row on back: K2, sl 1, K1, psso, K to last 4 sts, K2tog, K2. Cable panel B is used instead of cable panel A; this repeats over 20 rows instead of 10.

Back

Work as for cardigan with main part in st st.

Sleeves

Work as for cardigan, but with main part in st st (cable panel B).

Pockets

Omit.

Front

Work as for cardigan Back to **. Divide for neck and shape raglan armhole:

1st side

next row: cast off 4 sts, 1 st on r h needle, work 26(28, 30, 32, 34, 36) sts, turn. Work on these sts only.

foll row: work to end. Complete in the same way as Left Front of cardigan from *** to end.

2nd side

With r s of front facing, rejoin yarn at right of rem sts and complete the row.

next row: cast off 4 sts, work to end.

Complete to match 1st side, reversing shaping and reversing decs in the same way as for Right Front of cardigan.

Bands – Omit.

Neck edge

Join raglan seams taking in a seam of 1 st from each edge.

With r s of work facing, using dp sm needles, K up 16(16, 18, 18, 20, 20) sts from back neck, dec 1 st at each seam; K up 13 sts from top of sleeve, dec 1 st at each seam; pick up and K 34(36, 36, 38, 38, 40) sts from 1st side neck shaping and 35(37, 37, 39, 39, 41) sts from 2nd side neck shaping; and K up 13 sts from rem sleeve, dec 1 st at each seam.

111(115, 117, 121, 123, 127) sts. Mark centre front with a safety pin.

round 1: *K1 P1, repeat from * to 3 sts before pin, K1, K2tog, sl 1, K1, psso, *K1, P1, repeat from * to end.

round 2: *K1 P1, repeat from * to 2 sts before pin, K2tog, sl 1, K1, psso, *P1 K1 repeat from * to last st, P1.

Repeat these 2 rounds once more and round 1 once again.

Cast off in rib as set dec as for round 2 at centre front.

To make up

Join side and sleeve seams. Press according to instructions on ball bands.

Yarn stockists

For information on yarns or local stockists write to:

Argyll Wools

P.O. Box 15
Priestley Mills
Pudsey, W. Yorks.
LS28 9LT

Scotts Woolen Mill Inc.
528 Jefferson Avenue
Bristol, PA. 19007
USA

Avocet Yarns

The Bedford Wool Shop
The Old Arcade
Bedford, MK40 1NS
(mail order available)

Estelle Design & Sales Ltd
38 Continental Place
Scarborough
Ontario, M1R 2T4
Canada

Emu Wools

Leeds Road
Greengates
Bradford, BD10 9TE

The Plymouth Yarn Co.
P.O. Box 28
500 Lafayette Street
Bristol, PA. 19007
USA

Paton & Baldwins

Consumer Liaison Dept.
Alloa,
Clackmannanshire
Scotland FK10 1EG

Susan Bates Inc.
212 Middlesex Avenue
Chester, Ct 06412

Phildar Yarns

4 Gambrell Road
Westgate Estate
Northampton NN5 5NF

Ries Wools

243 High Holborn
London WC1
(mail order available)

6438 Dawson Boulevard
85 North,
Norcross, Ga 30093
USA

6200 Est.
Boulevard H. Hourassa,
Montreal NOrd, H1G 5X3
Canada

Pingouin Wools

French Wools Ltd
7/11 Lexington Street
London W1 4BU

Promafil Corp.
9170 Red Branch Road
Columbia, Md 21045
USA

Rowan Yarns

Green Lane Mill
Holmfirth
W. Yorks, HD7 1RW

Westminster Trading
5 Northern Boulevard
Amhurst, NH 03031
USA

Wendy Wools

Gordon Mills
Guiseley
W. Yorks LS20 9PD

White Buffalo Mills Ltd
45 Assiniboine Avenue
Brandon,
Manitoba, Canada R7A 0G3

Acknowledgements

hair stylist – Paula Mann at Simon Rattan

Page 34, trousers by Benetton and In-Wear; **page 35**, shorts by Walter van Beirdendonck; belt, Vanessa Schoen; **page 36**, grey satin pants, Benedetto; jewellery DN and Dickens and Jones; **page 38**, skirt, Benetton; tights, Next; **page 40**, white shirt, C17; trousers, Bennetton; **page 41**, beige shirt, John Elett; striped trousers, Benetton; jeans, Benetton; **page 45**, dress, Koko; **page 47**, knitted skirt, Benetton; hood, the Hat shop; **page 51**, broderie petticoat, Lunn Antiques; hat, The Hat Shop; **page 52**, hat, The Hat Shop; shirt, Lunn Antiques; **page 53**, boy's shirt and trousers, Benetton; cap, The Hat Shop; man's shirt and trousers, C17; **page 57**, white cotton trousers, Benetton; shirt, C17; French beret, The Hat Shop; belt, Vanessa Schoen; **page 58**, hat, Fred Bare at The Hat Shop; skirt and shirt, Stephen Linard; petticoat, Lunn Antiques.

INDEX

YARN REQUIREMENT GUIDE

This table sets out the average amount of yarn required for a long sleeved, classic fit, round neck sweater in stocking/stockinette stitch with 2″–3″ ease and at average tension/gauge (see also Tension/gauge chart on back endpapers). You will need more yarn for a more generous fit, complicated stitch pattern or patterns with more than one colour. To estimate these needs more precisely, see Calculating Yarn, page 16.

YARN	Approx. Metres per 50 gms	Approx. Yards per ounce	To fit child 26″ chest		To fit woman 34″ chest		To fit man 40″ chest	
			gms	ozs	gms	ozs	gms	ozs
2 PLY (LIGHT FINGERING)	450	230	150	6	250	9	300	11
3 PLY (FINGERING)	280	185	200	7	300	11	350	13
4 PLY (FINGERING/SPORT)	220	115	250	9	350	13	450	16
DOUBLE KNITTING (SPORT/KNITTING WORSTED)	135	70	300	11	400	15	500	18
ARAN	85	44	400	14	500	18	600	22
STANDARD MOHAIR	110	55	350	13	450	16	550	20
CHUNKY (BULKY)	80	42	450	15	550	20	700	25

NOTE:

1 metre (100 cms)	= 39½″
1 yard (36″)	= 91.5 cms
1 ounce	= 28 gms

004